Babygirl

INT. ROMY AND JACOB'S APARTMENT- BEDROOM NIGHT

Close on: a woman's face, ROMY (49). Pure ecstasy. She holds her breath, lets go and and starts to orgasm. The camera reveals her husband JACOB (58, warm, handsome) who is laying underneath her and climaxes at the same time. He is in heaven as she leans down and brings her face close to his.

JACOB
I love you.

ROMY
(warm)
Love you.

Lovingly, she kisses him. He turns over and falls asleep. A beat. Romy's eyes are restless. Quietly, she gets out of bed.

INT. ROMY AND JACOB'S APARTMENT- LONG HALLWAY TO BEDROOMS - NIGHT

Quickly, Romy walks to her study.

INT. ROMY AND JACOB'S APARTMENT- STUDY NIGHT

Romy sneaks into her study, and opens her laptop. The screen lights up the otherwise dark room. She types quickly, then takes the laptop from the desk, and puts it down on the floor. She lies down on her belly in front of it. She faces the computer. She clicks on one of the video's. Her hand moves towards her crotch. On the screen Romy sees:

Close on a WOMAN's face. She answers questions from a man who is filming her.

MAN
(whispers)
How does daddy use you?

WOMAN
Anyway he pleases..

MAN
Louder.

WOMAN
Any way he pleases.

Romy sees how the couple on her screen start to have rough sex. She covers her mouth with her hand, while she pleasures herself until she comes. **For real this time.**

Immediately after she climaxes, she closes the laptop. The room goes dark.

Over black, the title:

BABYGIRL

INT. AUTOMATED WAREHOUSE-DAY

<u>An overhead shot of a fully automated warehouse.</u> **<u>Robots are driving over a system of rails and magnetic tape, picking and placing products in thousands of boxes. It is as if we are looking inside Romy's head.</u>**

INT. ROMY AND JACOB'S APARTMENT BATHROOM-EARLY MORNING

Close on Romy's face. She applies toner, hyaluronic acid, day-cream. She uses a Dermaflash tool to smoothen her skin. She plucks her eyebrows. She taps her face with her fingers. She applies bright pink blush to her cheeks. A mask of make up. As she goes through her routine, she practices a speech.

          ROMY
     (mumbling quietly)
  Unmatched order, accuracy and
  efficiency....to transform
  warehouses into future ready
  opportunity centers....An increase
  in e-commerce and fast shipping
  expectations- in the face of real
  estate and labour shortages...

INT. ROMY AND JACOB'S APARTMENT- KITCHEN EARLY MORNING

Classical music is playing. Before anyone wakes up, Romy sets the breakfast table perfectly. She is wearing an apron. Carefully, she prepares lunch boxes. She sits down to write little notes for her daughters. She hides them in their backpacks.

                                      CUT TO:

Romy is serving pancakes. Her two daughters, ISABEL (15) and NORA (13) sit at the table. Jacob is on the phone with an actor joking and discussing the character of *Lovborg* in Hedda Gabler. In front of him on the table, paper and a red pen. Everyone is talking at once. We hear fragments of Jacob's phone conversation.

                    JACOB
          Because Hedda wants him to end his
          life courageously, romantically-

                    ISABEL
          So what are you going to wear?

                    ISABEL (CONT'D)
                (laughing)
          Did you give them to Ed?

                    ROMY
          Who's Ed?

                    NORA
          The homeless woman downstairs-

          JACOB   NORA (CONT'D)
     (into the phone)   I don't need them. I'm a
Exactly! Show that you're   dancer not a hiker.
showing!

                    ISABEL
                (laughing)
          We always hike, so you do need
          them.

                    JACOB
                (smiling, to his wife)
          Why do you keep wearing that?

Romy looks at her apron. Jacob takes the pen and paper from
the table and walks away, laughing at a joke the actor makes
on the phone.

          ROMY   ISABEL
     (to Jacob about the   (to her sister)
       apron)   You can't come if you don't
You don't like it?   have hiking shoes. We'll
                               leave you behind.

                    ROMY (CONT'D)
                (to Nora)
          The ones we bought last month? Did
          you give them away?

                    NORA
          Yes. They made me look weird.

                    ROMY
          To a homeless person?

                    ISABEL
          Ed.

> ROMY
> Did he fit them?

> NORA
> She.

> ROMY
> She!

> ISABEL
> Can Mary spend the night?

> ROMY
> (Decisive)
> No!

Nora starts to move through the kitchen to practice the tarantella. Automatically, Romy guides her back to her chair.

> ISABEL
> Why?

Jacob looks at Isabel and quickly hangs up.

> JACOB
> Your mother is busy with her company right now. So we need peace and quiet- It's a scary time.

> ROMY
> (laughing)
> It's not scary, it's exciting!

> ISABEL
> (imitating her mother's smile)
> It's not scary it's exciting!

Jacob laughs. Romy, a bit offended, touches her necklace. Jacob hands her the piece of paper with her speech on it.

> JACOB
> I made some small changes.

Playfully, Jacob grabs his wife and makes her giggle.

EXT. BUSY STREET IN MIDTOWN NEW YORK DAY

Romy walks down a very busy street. Suddenly, someone starts to scream. People rush towards her. Anxious, she looks up to see what they are running from. A barking DOG with wild eyes runs towards her. People try to get away. Someone hides behind a car. A man in a business suit tries to stop the dog.

>   MACHO MAN
>   (loud)
>   Hey! Calm the fuck down!

His voice only makes the animal more scared and disorientated. The dog focusses his attention on a child. Romy jumps in front of it. For a moment it seems hypnotized by Romy's fearlessness, but then it suddenly jumps on top of her, causing her to trip and fall. Before it can bite her, it is distracted by a whistling sound. The dog walks away from her, into the direction of <u>A YOUNG MAN, SAMUEL</u> (25, in a cheap suit and coat that seem too big for him) He looks straight into the eyes of the dog, and holds out his hand. Abruptly, it stops barking and walks curiously toward the hand. While Romy gets herself together, she tries to see what's going on through the legs of the people around her.

EXT. / INT.   OFFICE BUILDING ENTRANCE/ LOBBY- DAY

Romy rushes in. Someone is hanging decorations on a large, beautiful Christmas tree. ESME, Romy's assistant (25), comes running.

INT. OFFICE BUILDING HALLWAY / MEETING ROOM DAY

Romy walks down the stairs in the middle of the busy office. Esme follows carrying Romy's bag and laptop.

>   ROMY (PRE-LAP)
>   Humans are the most ethical beings
>   on the face of the earth, but also
>   the least ethical. The state of our
>   planet proves it.

INT. OFFICE BUILDING PRESS ROOM DAY

On a screen behind Romy we see large mobile robots, picking and placing products from shelves into boxes and containers. The logo of her company: **Tensile Automation,** is projected over the images. She speaks into a small camera. A live stream of a product launch. Romy is introducing new robot called Harvest. Some employees, technicians, and HAZEL (46, head of marketing) are watching. A make up station, a clothing rack and craft services table.

                    ROMY
          As more and more artificial
          intelligence is entering into the
          world, more and more emotional
          intelligence must enter into
          leadership." We are living through
          an era of historic transformation,
          unlocking sustainable, inclusive
          growth in new sectors of the
          economy. We are making the
          workplace, healthier, safer and
          more productive. We engineer
          accountability into our products
          and they are changing the way we
          live, every day.
          I am delighted to introduce to you,
          the newest asset to our fleet:
          HARVEST

She smiles into the camera. *Music starts playing.*

INT. OFFICE BUILDING ROMY'S OFFICE DAY

Esme knocks on the door and pops her head in. Romy jumps up and tries to fix her hair.

                    ROMY
               (smiling)
          Response is great I hear.

                    ESME
               (genuinely enthusiastic)
          Yes! The quote about emotional
          intelligence was very-

                    ROMY
          Jacob's idea.

                    ESME
          Is this a good time for me to
          introduce the... interns-

                    ROMY
               (without thinking)
          Now is good!

Through the glass we see a group of interns.

                    ESME
          It's their first day so-

Romy nods. Esme opens the door and lets the small group of young men and women enter, among them Samuel.

                    ROMY   ESME (CONT'D)
            (enthusiastically)   This is our CEO, Romy Mathis!
    Hello!

    No one speaks. Romy takes off her reading glasses. She smiles
    kindly.

                              ROMY (CONT'D)
                    Don't be nervous...Welcome! We are
                    so very happy to have you with us.

    Relieved they smile back.

                              ROMY (CONT'D)
                    If you have any questions, let us
                    know.

    She looks back at her laptop as a sign that they can leave.
    Suddenly Samuel, hidden behind the other interns, in the back
    of the room, raises his hand.

                              SAMUEL
                    I have a question.

    Romy looks up. To her surprise she recognizes him as the boy
    who calmed the dog down earlier that morning.

                              SAMUEL (CONT'D)
                        (without taking his eyes
                         off of her)
                    Do you really believe that
                    automation can provide a path to
                    sustainability or is that just
                    something people say to make you
                    like robots?

    He smiles. Before Romy can answer, Esme quickly interrupts.

                              ESME
                    Ok! Lets go, Mrs. Mathis is very
                    busy today.

    She guides the interns to the door. Romy stares at Samuel.

                              INTERN ROSE
                        (In Samuel's ear)
                    It's her company.

    Samuel nods and smiles. Quickly, Esme escorts the group out.
    Before Esme pushes him through the door, Samuel looks back at
    Romy. Romy's phone starts to ring. Before she leaves Esme
    says:

                    ESME
          I am so sorry about that, do you
          want me to- (get rid of him?)

Romy isn't listening. She answers her phone.

                    ROMY
               (into the phone)
          Yes?(...) Oh! Of course (...) we
          should dissect that a little though-
          It was an excellent day... a very
          successful beginning-

Through the glass walls of her office, we see the interns
walk away. Samuel keeps his eyes on Romy.

INT. OFFICE BUILDING 6TH FLOOR NIGHT

The group of interns are getting a tour of the building.
Everyone is talking over each other. Tom and Esme explain how
the internship works and point out different area's of the
office. Esme hands out bags with welcome packages. Samuel
takes it all in.

                    INTERN ANNA
          So who can apply for it?

                    ESME
          For what?

Everyone quiets down and listens.

                    TOM
          Everyone. It's a company wide
          program. You'll receive a list of
          names by email at the end of the
          day.

                    ESME
          I highly recommend it. A mentor
          makes a huge difference in how you
          get to experience the company.

                    TOM
          And you're all invited to the
          holiday party this Friday.

                    ESME
          There will be a DJ, make sure you
          bring your dancing shoes!

Everyone laughs and talks over each other.

INT. OFFICE BUILDING ELEVATOR- DAY

The next morning, Romy walks into the elevator. A group of men in suits look at her.

                    ARI
          Good Morning Mrs. Mathis.

                    ROMY
          Good morning Ari.

INT. OFFICE BUILDING MEETING ROOM- LATE MORNING

Romy holds court for a group of business men.

                    ROMY (PRE-LAP)
          He's a problem... and we don't need
          him...

INT. OFFICE BUILDING DESKS/ 6TH FLOOR STAIRS/ CANTEEN COFFEE MACHINE- DAY

Romy, with her coat on, walks through the office, she is on the phone looking for someone.

                    ROMY
          Exactly...that's what I told him...
          Investors appetite is huge...

As she passes people's desks they look up from their screens. She turns a corner and sees Samuel drinking water at the coffee machine. Rose (Intern) is saying goodbye to him. As Rose leaves:

                    ROMY (CONT'D)
               (to Samuel)
          Hey- Could you make me a coffee?

Quickly, Samuel nods and takes a cup from a shelf.

                    ROMY (CONT'D)
               (into the phone)
          Right- safe navigation,
          flexibility...real time
          monitoring...
               (while looking at Samuel)
          Technology alone wont solve that
          though- Yes, okay- Talk later.

She hangs up as he hands her the coffee. She looks straight into his eyes.

                    ROMY (CONT'D)
          How did you get that dog to calm
          down?

He observes her for a beat.

                    SAMUEL
              (without blinking)
          I gave it a cookie.

She raises her eyebrows.

                    ROMY
          You always have cookies on you?

He smiles and nods.

                    SAMUEL
          Yeah.
              (he looks at her with a
               twinkle in his eyes)
          Why?

He sticks his hand in his pocket.

                    SAMUEL (CONT'D)
              (cheeky)
          Do you want one?

She shakes her head.

                    ROMY
              (serious)
          No.

For a brief moment he sees an unexpected vulnerability in her eyes. He tilts his head, like an animal.

                    SAMUEL
              (fatherly)
          You shouldn't drink coffee after
          lunch. How many do you drink a day?

                    ROMY
          None of your business.
              (pause)
          Seven.

They stand there silently for several seconds until her phone rings, breaking the tension.

                                ROMY (CONT'D)
                        (into the phone but still
                        looking at Samuel)
                    Yes?

She walks away.

INT. ROMY AND JACOB'S APARTMENT BEDROOM- NIGHT

In the dark, in bed, Romy watches business news on her phone.
Jacob turns towards her and gently touches her shoulder.

                                JACOB
                    I want to see you.

He switches the light on. Romy looks away.

                                JACOB (CONT'D)
                        (whispers)
                    Look at me. Hey, hey look at me...

Romy playfully disappears under the sheets. She sits there
fully covered by the sheet like a ghost. Her childish
behavior makes him laugh. She speaks from under the sheets.

                                ROMY
                        (whispers, shy)
                    I want you to watch porn while you
                    have sex with me.

He thinks he didn't hear her correctly.

                                JACOB
                    What?

                                ROMY
                    I want to-

Embarrassed, she stops herself.

                                JACOB
                    Ok-

Romy giggles. Jacob starts to kiss her through the sheet.

                                ROMY
                    -feels weird.

Smiling, she takes the sheet away and lays on her back. She
grabs a pillow and puts it over her face. He stares at the
pillow. He shakes his head. Romy speaks from under the
pillow.

                              ROMY (CONT'D)
                         (softly, with a baby
                          voice)
                    You touch me.

He starts to caress her body.

                              ROMY (CONT'D)
                    No. Like this. You touch me.

She puts the pillow back over her head. He tries to caress
her again. He kisses her breasts. She moans.

                              ROMY (CONT'D)
                    Yes. Do it.

He moves away.

                              ROMY (CONT'D)
                         (from under the pillow)
                    Come on- Do it-

                              JACOB
                         (smiles)
                    You know I can't- Like this.

She doesn't take the pillow away. He sighs.

                              JACOB (CONT'D)
                    It makes me feel like ...a villain.

                              ROMY
                    Okay...okay.

She takes the pillow away and kisses him. She tries to
surrender to him. Very gently they start to make love. Jacob
looks at her, she tries to keep her eyes focused on his.

INT. OFFICE BUILDING PRESS ROOM- DAY

Close on Romy, she looks straight into the camera.

                              ROMY
                    Being a CEO is- being a
                    collaborator- a nurturer. I see
                    myself as a strategy expert but
                    also- a human expert.

They are rehearsing for a press day. Esme is typing on her
phone. HAZEL is drilling Romy.

                    ROMY (CONT'D)
          At the same time, one day shipping
          dramatically upped the stakes. The
          demand for what we do is huge.
          People are waiting for us to buckle
          under that pressure. The best thing
          to do is, smile and look up. Never
          show your weakness-

                    HAZEL
               (interrupts her)
          Don't use "weakness" to describe
          yourself. It's a positive to be
          vulnerable, not a negative-

Romy nods her head.

                    ROMY
          Got it.

She smiles.

INT. OFFICE BUILDING 6TH FLOOR - END OF DAY

The office Christmas party. Music is playing. Everyone is
having a good time. Romy and Esme welcome Jacob and the
children. Isabel feels awkward in her girly dress. Nora is
comfortably wearing a princess dress. Immediately, they are
surrounded by people who want to greet Romy's family. Female
employees try to get close to Jacob.

INT. OFFICE BUILDING 6TH FLOOR   NIGHT

Later-Esme and Romy sit in a quiet corner. Esme is tipsy.

                    ROMY
          Did you hear about those murders
          uptown?

Esme nods.

                    ROMY (CONT'D)
          Do you think a woman would be
          capable of killing so many young
          men?

                    ESME
          It's really good to like think
          about death more.

                    ROMY
          What?

                    ESME
          I mean, to like bring awareness to
          death more? Like that Buddhist
          quote. "We don't give enough
          attention to the avalanche that
          will cover us all, in a very short
          time."

                    ROMY
          Well, you're still an embryo, so
          you shouldn't think about death at
          all! Leave that to us dinosaurs.

                    ESME
          Can I ask you- Where does your
          first name come from? Is it Polish?

Romy observes her for a beat.

                    ROMY
               (bluntly)
          I was named by a guru.

                    ESME
          What?? Seriously? How? When?

                    ROMY
          I was raised in cults and communes.

Romy studies Esme's face to check her reaction.

                    ESME
               (smiling, a bit tipsy)
          You were? I would have NEVER
          guessed. I thought you were raised
          by soldiers or something. Or
          robots!

Romy looks at her.

                    ESME (CONT'D)
               (afraid she overstepped)
          I mean- I'm joking, of course.

Samuel walks by, he makes eye contact with Romy.

                    ROMY
          Did you know him before?

Esme shakes her head and takes another sip from her wine.

                    ESME
          Do you think I'm too young for
          fillers?

                    ROMY
          Why?

                    ESME
          Barbara said I have a gummy smile.

                    ROMY
          Who? That's insane, I hope you
          realize that.

Realizing how ridiculous it is, Esme smiles. Romy laughs.

EXT. OFFICE BUILDING TERRACE-NIGHT

In her coat, Romy is alone smoking a cigarette. Suddenly Samuel appears.

                    SAMUEL
          Do you have a lighter?

She hands him one. He lights his cigarette. They smoke and look at the city below them, flickering with Christmas lights.

                    SAMUEL (CONT'D)
              (kind)
          I don't like Christmas. Do you?

She thinks about the question. After a beat, they start talking at the same time.

          ROMY   SAMUEL (CONT'D)
I have no- issues with it.   You know what I read-

                    SAMUEL (CONT'D)
          Sorry, you go first.

                    ROMY
              (smiles)
          No. You... Go.

They are quiet. He stares into her eyes. She doesn't look away.

                    SAMUEL
              (as if he just remembered)
          Oh! I chose you as my mentor.

                    ROMY
          What?

                    SAMUEL
          I chose you as my mentor.

She shakes her head while blowing out smoke.

                ROMY
I'm not a part of that program.

                SAMUEL
You are.

                ROMY
No I'm not.

                SAMUEL
          (without taking his eyes
           off of her)
You are. You're on the list. I got an email and I clicked on your name.
          (he smiles, a beat)
So- You're on the list.

Samuel stubs out his cigarette.

                SAMUEL (CONT'D)
Thank you for the light.

He walks away. Puzzled, Romy stays behind.

INT. OFFICE BUILDING 6TH FLOOR   NIGHT

Later- people are dancing. Jacob is dancing with Nora and Isabel. Nora tries to get her mother to join but she shakes her head. MR. MISSEL (73, board of directors, fatherly) and Romy's eyes meet. He smiles at her refusal to dance with her family. In a corner of the room, the interns talk to each other. Samuel dances with an older woman. Romy watches him. He takes off his jacket and tie. As he dances, his tie falls to the ground.

INT. ROMY AND JACOB'S APARTMENT KITCHEN- NIGHT

Later that night- At home Jacob eats from a tub of Greek vanilla yoghurt. The Hedda Gabler script in front of him. Romy is typing on her phone.

                JACOB
Scarlett doesn't understand Hedda Gabler at all - She thinks it's about desire. It's not about desire, It's about suicide.

                    ROMY
               (distracted)
          OK.

Romy looks at her phone.

                    JACOB
               (changing the subject back
                to Hedda)
          Hedda's life is over before the
          play begins-

                    ROMY
               (eyes fixated on her
                screen, very distracted)
          Right- Yes. Before it begins. It's-
          over. That makes- a lot of sense-
          to me.

                    JACOB
          What are you mumbling about? You're
          not saying any words- are you
          having a seizure?

She laughs. She loves him when he teases her.

                    ROMY
               (laughing)
          You're so rude-

                    JACOB
               (flirty)
          Who are you texting the whole time?

                    ROMY
               (smiles)
          When I'm on my phone it's for work.
          Especially now -you know that.

                    JACOB
               (laughs)
          As if that's a good excuse! That's
          the whole problem!

He laughs.

                    JACOB (CONT'D)
          Hey, come here.

He takes her in his arms. He looks into her eyes.

                    JACOB (CONT'D)
                (half smiling, half
                 vulnerable)
           Am I-- relevant to you as a
           director?

                    ROMY
           Everyone is irrelevant. We don't
           give enough attention to the
           avalanche that will cover us all,
           in a very short time.

                    JACOB
           What?

They both laugh. He kisses her. They hug.

INT. OFFICE BUILDING HALLWAY - DAY

The next morning- it's Saturday. Romy, with her coat on, looks around. A caterer wheels out a cart of glassware. A deflated balloon on the floor. The office is empty. A cleaner is vacuuming. Romy takes a water from the fridge when out of the corner of her eye, she spots Samuel's tie on the floor next to where everyone was dancing. She picks it up and puts it in her bag.

INT. OFFICE BUILDING ROMY'S OFFICE DAY

Later- Romy is working on her laptop with her coat still on. Business news plays loudly. She tries to focus but keeps looking at her bag on the edge of the sofa. Hesitant, she gets up. She lowers the blinds, to make sure no one can see her. She sits down on the sofa. Unsure of herself, she takes the tie out of her bag. She looks around before she smells it. Slowly, she brings the tie to her mouth. Her hand moves towards her skirt. She pushes the tie deeper into her mouth while she starts to touch herself.

INT. REMEDY PLACE-DAY

Close up of Romy's face. A needle is penetrating her upper lip. Romy gets Botox and fillers. It hurts but she doesn't mind.

                    DOCTOR
           You sure you don't want some
           numbing cream?

She shakes her head.

INT. REMEDY PLACE- DAY

Romy lies in a hyperbaric oxygen chamber and works on her I-Pad.

Romy submerges her body in a ice cold plunge tank.

Romy does cryotherapy wearing ear protectors , a black bathing suit and large gloves. Her breath is visible in the cold.

INT. EMDR THERAPY CLINIC/ UNDEFINED SPACES - DAY

Close on Romy's face with headphones on. We hear the sound of Audio Bilateral stimulation moving from our left ear to our right. Up close we see her eyes move from left to right, following a light-bar. Her wrists are stimulated every few seconds by vibrating black wristbands, which she wears like handcuffs.

> THERAPIST
> 5,4,3,2,1...

Romy closes her eyes. Flashback to: Romy's childhood. A group of children dance wildly.

> THERAPIST (CONT'D)
> What do you feel?

Close on her eyes moving rapidly. We see a flash of Samuel's hands, feeding a treat to the dog on the street.

> ROMY
> Nothing.

A flash of the dog standing over Romy as she lays on the street on her back.

> THERAPIST
> No feelings in your body?

INT. ROMY AND JACOB'S APARTMENT- LIVING ROOM- DAY

Through the lens of the photographer we see the family posing for their yearly Christmas card picture next to their tastefully decorated Christmas tree. A perfect American nuclear family except for the fact that Nora is wearing her traditional Tarantella dance dress, and Isabel is in an oversized hoody with a scary print . The photographer is taking the shot, when suddenly Romy isn't able to restrain herself any longer, and jumps up.

She pushes the photographer out of the way, stands behind the
camera and looks through the lens.

                    ROMY
      Well- ok. We've got that-
         (kindly)
      Would you go change now Isabel,
      please?

                    JACOB
      Romy, come on. Jesus-

           ROMY   JACOB (CONT'D)
You look beautiful, and we   Let them wear what they want!
have this shot, but it's not
the style we are going for.
It's not what we agreed upon.

                ROMY (CONT'D)
         (with a smile)
      Go change please.

Suddenly, Isabel starts laughing.

                   ISABEL
      Your face looks really weird!

Romy touches her lips. Her heart sinks. Nora looks at her mom
and bursts out laughing too.

                ISABEL (CONT'D)
         (laughing)
      You look like a dead fish!

Hurt and embarrassed, Romy looks away.

                   JACOB
      Isabel!

                  ISABEL
      Sorry dad, but she looks awful!
         (to her mom)
      Why do you do that to yourself?!

Isabel storms off.

                   ROMY
         (friendly, to Nora)
      Baby, will you go get changed now
      please?

Nora nods and leaves. Jacob gives his wife a look. Romy
smiles.

> ROMY (CONT'D)
> (to the photographer)
> Ok! Why don't you take one of the two of us while we're waiting for them to change?

She smiles. Romy and Jacob pose together.

INT. OFFICE BUILDING ELEVATOR DAY

Monday morning; Romy walks into the elevator trying to hide a small bruise caused by the fillers. The bruise is covered by concealer, which makes it look worse. Self-conscious she touches it.

> SAMUEL O. S
> Wait - hold the door-

Samuel walks in. Romy stands with her back against the wall. Samuel stands next to her, at a respectful distance. She looks at their reflection in the closing doors, she tries to hide her face behind her hair. He looks at her.

> SAMUEL
> I'm looking forward to Tuesday.

> ROMY
> (confused)
> Sorry?

> SAMUEL
> I got an email saying they scheduled the first session.

> ROMY
> The what?

> SAMUEL
> The ten minute introduction meeting?

She looks at him as if he has lost his mind.

> ROMY
> (trying to be polite)
> I have no idea who sent you that email but they'll have to find someone else. I don't have time.

> SAMUEL
> It's just ten minutes-
> (he tilts his head and
> stares at the bruise)

He points at her cheek.

                    SAMUEL (CONT'D)
        What's that?

                    ROMY
           (pretending not to know)
        What's what?

He points at his own face.

                    SAMUEL
        There's no need for the-

Embarrassed she looks away.

                    SAMUEL (CONT'D)
        Looks good on you.

With a *loud ding* the elevator stops. Blushing, she walks out. Tom is waiting for her in the hallway. He stares at Samuel through the elevator doors. Samuel stares back as the doors close in front of him.

EXT/INT   OFFICE TERRACE/ MEETING ROOM -DUSK

Esme sits alone on a bench. Samuel walks up to her and sits down next to her. They talk and laugh.

From a window high above, Romy watches them.

INT. OFFICE BUILDING ROMY'S OFFICE- NIGHT

Esme is applying more concealer to Romy's bruise.

                    ROMY
        Who decided that I'm part of that
        mentor program by the way?

                    ESME
        Hazel thought it would be good for
        you to take part in some extra
        activities internally... They say
        there's a talent war-so I guess
        it's important to make new talent
        feel involved. Show you're an
        approachable leader-

                    ROMY
        Yes- The talent war-

They both laugh.

> ESME
> You think we can talk about my promotion soon?

> ROMY
> (warm)
> Of course-

Romy checks herself in a hand mirror.

EXT. NEW YORK CITY- EARLY MORNING.

From high above, the sun rises over the skyline.

INT. OFFICE BASEMENT HALLWAY- DAY

Romy walks along the empty hallway, towards basement meeting room.

INT. OFFICE BUILDING WINDOWLESS BASEMENT ROOM- DAY

Nervous and excited, Samuel sits at a table, with a yellow pad and a pen, waiting. A long beat before Romy comes in.

> ROMY
> You have seven minutes.

> SAMUEL
> Ten.

He gets up to shake her hand, but she ignores him.

> SAMUEL (CONT'D)
> Thank you so much for making the time.

> ROMY
> (mumbles)
> I was forced.

> SAMUEL
> Excuse me?

She gives him a look.

> SAMUEL (CONT'D)
> Why did you want to meet here?

                    ROMY
          You don't like this room?

                    SAMUEL
          No. I do. It's perfect.

He feels the wall.

                    SAMUEL (CONT'D)
          It's soundproof.

She stares at him, not knowing what to think.

                    ROMY
          I would hurry up if I were you.

                    SAMUEL
          Of course. So--- how- did- it-
          start?

                    ROMY
          What?

                    SAMUEL
          The warehouse automation dream?
          It's an interesting choice
          considering the climate crisis.

                    ROMY
          That's your question? Google it.

                    SAMUEL
          I want to hear it from you.

                    ROMY
          Why?

                    SAMUEL
          Cause the internet is unreliable.

Briefly she looks into his eyes. Then she starts to speak at a very fast pace.

                    ROMY
          I graduated from Yale cum laude and
          was recruited by an investment
          firm. The selection process was
          gruesome. There were six rooms, and
          in every room, I had to answer
          certain questions and solve math
          formulas. One of the questions was
          how many ping pong balls would fit
          in that specific room.

SAMUEL
How many ping pong balls fit in this room?

She ignores him.

ROMY
At the end they gave me a hypothetical case of a company that was in deep trouble, and I had to figure out how to make them profitable again. For a week I tried to solve it, but I couldn't, so I went in and told them they could go fuck themselves-

SAMUEL
What did they say?

ROMY
They hired me.

SAMUEL
Because you were bold?

ROMY
I guess they were looking for certain personalities.

SAMUEL
What kind?

ROMY
(ignoring him)
I started my own company five years later with the goal to change the global supply chain forever. I wanted to automate repetitive tasks, to give people their time back so they can spend it in a fulfilling way-

SAMUEL
(interrupting her)
Power hungry personalities?

ROMY
You think that's what I am?

SAMUEL
No, the opposite.

ROMY
You think I don't like power?

                    SAMUEL
               (soft)
          No. I think you like to be told
          what to do.

The air the leaves the room. Samuel blushes, shocked at his
own words. Romy freezes.

                    SAMUEL (CONT'D)
          Sorry. I didn't mean to- that's
          inappropriate - that's incredibly
          inappropriate-

He smiles. Embarrassed, he looks at his yellow pad. He starts
to write. She stares at his hand moving extremely fast over
the paper, writing down all kinds of numbers. Suddenly she
grabs the pen out of hid hand. Surprised, he looks up. He
smiles as if he recognizes something. She <u>writes down her
phone number on his yellow pad</u>, before she hands the pen back
to him.

                    ROMY
               (explaining herself,
                trying to sound
                indifferent)
          Seven minutes are up, but we can do
          another session- if that's what you
          were hoping for...

With kind eyes he looks at her phone number, and then at her.

                    SAMUEL
               (about the phone number)
          I already have it.

Confused she starts to walk to the door.

                    SAMUEL (CONT'D)
               (about the ping pong
                balls))
          818007, is the answer.

Without looking back at him, she opens the door to leave.
Suddenly, he stands behind her. He slowly closes the door.
She lets him. She turns around to face him. Her lips are
almost touching his. Their mouths gradually near each other.

                    ROMY
          I have to go.

When her lips almost touch his, he pulls back. Her breathing
sounds loud. They stand like that for a while, until she
can't control herself any longer. Suddenly, she kisses him.

Surprised by her warm lips, her hungry, open mouth, Samuel freezes, then heat spreads through his body, and he thaws. He kisses her back. Long. Until she stops. They are both confused by what just happened.

> ROMY (CONT'D)
> (embarrassed)
> I'm so sorry, I shouldn't have done that.

> SAMUEL
> (kind)
> It's ok. It's fine.

> ROMY
> It's not ok. I am so sorry.

> SAMUEL
> It's ok-

He smiles. Slowly realizing what she has done, she stares at him, petrified. She forces a smile on her face and changes her tone.

> ROMY
> Great! Ok! Thank you!

He looks at her with warm eyes.

> SAMUEL
> Thank you.

She leaves.

Pre-lap: *A LOUD SCREAM.*

> NORA
> Moooooooooooommmm! Mom!

EXT. UPSTATE HOUSE - DAY

From high in the sky, the camera slowly moves in on the perfect family (Romy, Jacob, Isabel and Nora). They walk towards their perfect family home. The lights are on inside, lit up like a doll's house.

INT. UPSTATE HOUSE BEDROOM- NIGHT

Romy and Jacob are sleeping. Her phone buzzes. Romy wakes up. She doesn't recognize the number. She hears a sound. She looks at Jacob, who is still sleeping. Anxious, she gets out of bed. She walks up to the window.

To her surprise, she sees Isabel in the pool with A GIRL (OPHELIA, 17). Steam comes off of the heated water. It's a magical image. They kiss. Romy wants to go downstairs but instead she just watches, entranced. She looks back at her phone.

IN. UPSTATE HOUSE BEDROOM- EARLY MORNING

The family sleeps together in a huge bed. Nora cuddles a teddy bear. Peaceful. Isabel, at the foot of the bed, in her bathing suit and pajama pants.

EXT. UPSTATE HOUSE SWIMMING POOL- DAY

With a net Romy tries to fish a small dead skunk out of the pool. Isabel comes to help her, trying to connect to Romy. They manage to hoist the dead animal onto the edge.

    ROMY
 Do you like the girl from next
 door? How old is she, 17?

Surprised Isabel looks up.

    ISABEL
  (blushing)
 What do you mean?

    ROMY
 I thought you were in love with-
 Mary?

Isabel studies her face. She notices her mother's vulnerability.

    ISABEL
  (patiently explaining)
 I am in love with Mary -I'm just
 having fun with Ophelia.

Romy looks at her daughter, a bit confused.

INT. OFFICE BUILDING MEETING ROOM/ BULLPEN -DAY

Full screen: a video on proper conduct in the workplace. Samuel and some other interns make notes. Through the glass wall, he sees Romy speaking to her team next to a big monitor that plays a video of the warehouses. Esme stands next to her. Romy seems angry. He studies her dominant body language and facial expressions. He watches her as she puts on her coat and leaves. Samuel gets up.

INT./ EXT. OFFICE BUILDING LOBBY TO PLAZA- DAY

Romy walks out of the office, Samuel comes running after her.

SAMUEL
(polite)
Hey! Wait! Sorry- Can I ask you something?

Romy keeps walking.

SAMUEL (CONT'D)
Why didn't you respond?

ROMY
To what?

She increases her speed but he keeps walking next to her. Christmas lights everywhere.

SAMUEL
They said we are supposed to meet weekly, but you didn't answer the email. They sent an email.

ROMY
I have to go- I have an appointment.

He stands in front of her. Nervous, she looks around to see if anyone is watching them.

SAMUEL
(patiently explaining)
It's very easy. The email has a link. You just click on a date and a time for the second appointment-
It will pop up in your calendar-

ROMY
I have to go.

But she doesn't move. He tilts his head, he takes a step towards her. He shifts his tone.

SAMUEL
Listen, if you don't want to be my mentor, I totally understand.
(he smiles)
I'll ask someone else, but I do want one. They say it makes a huge difference. There's lots of other people I can ask, so-

                    ROMY
          Are you done?

                    SAMUEL
          With?

She brings her face close to his.

                    ROMY
               (whispers)
          Do you understand that your
          behavior is totally out of line?

                    SAMUEL
          Is it?

Their bodies are close, she looks at him. They take each
other in. She can smell him. The tension is building, their
faces are just inches apart. She wants to leave but she can't
bring herself to walk away from him.

                    SAMUEL (CONT'D)
          We are supposed to meet once a
          week, that's how it works. I didn't
          make the rules.

People are walking past them. With big eyes she looks at him.
She smiles.

                    ROMY
          Ok. Yes. I'll think about it.

She turns around and walks away. Her cheeks are red. The
streets of New York are busy. The loud sounds of the city
overwhelm her. Her head is spinning. She looks up.

PRE-LAB:

BANG! BANG!

INT. THEATER- DAY

BANG! Loud shots are fired straight at the camera.

                    HEDDA (SCARLETT)
               (loud, with joy)
          *This is what comes of sneaking in
          by the back-way!*

HEDDA (SCARLETT, 32) holds a pistol and fires again.

                    BRACK (STEPHEN)
          Are you out of your senses?

From behind the audience seats, judge BRACK is making his way to the stage. Romy walks in, trying to be invisible. For a moment Scarlett (Hedda) looks at Romy. Behind Scarlett we see on a huge video wall, Scarlett's face.

> HEDDA
> (laughing)
> *Dear me, did I happen to hit you?*

Brack climbs onto the stage, and aggressively takes the pistol from her hand. Before she can speak, he points it at her forehead. Scarlett leans into the gun. Romy stands in the back. She holds her breath. She sees herself in Hedda.

> BRACK
> *I wish you would leave these pranks alone.*

Quietly, Romy takes a seat behind her husband who is rehearsing. Next to him two assistants and their laptops. Surprised, and a bit taken aback, Jacob turns around.

> JACOB
> (whispers)
> What are you doing here?

> BRACK
> *You're not really happy. That's the bottom of it.*

On stage, the actors stop.

> SCARLETT
> (To Stephen. Not realizing
> her mic is still on)
> What's going on?

The mics are muted.

> ROMY
> (whispers to Jacob)
> Watching you in your natural habitat.

> JACOB
> The last time you did that was in 1997 when you thought I was having an affair with a light technician.

Romy laughs. He looks at her red cheeks.

> JACOB (CONT'D)
> You don't have to be at work?

She smiles. Jacob gets up to give directions. Romy briefly grabs his hand. She looks at him full of admiration, before he runs towards the stage. Fascinated, Romy watches Jacob. Seeing him work reminds her how much she loves him.

INT. LUXURIOUS BAR MIDTOWN- NIGHT

A bar filled with loud business men in suits. Romy walks in with Hazel, Tom and Robert. They pass a group of interns and young employees. Samuel looks at Romy as she walks by. Romy ignores him. Surprised to see Romy entering the bar, Esme jumps up. The young people around Esme start to whisper in each others ears when they notice Romy. Romy and her team take a seat at a table in the back. Esme comes over.

                    ESME
               (A bit tipsy)
         You finally came! We've been
         begging her to get a drink with us
         for over a year!

Everyone laughs. Esme sits down next to Hazel.

                  ESME (CONT'D)
         You know what we should focus on
         way more? Recruiting women.
         Especially young female engineers-

                  HAZEL
         Oh, trust me, we are.

Samuel watches Romy from the bar.

                  ESME
         I know, but wouldn't it be cool to
         offer, like, a special support
         program within the company for
         young female employees? So they can
         find their way to the top easier?

                  ROMY
               (to Hazel)
         Listen to her!

                  HAZEL
         We would love to sit down and
         discuss that with you.

                  ESME
         You would?

Proud, Esme looks at Romy. Charmed by Esme's drunken enthusiasm, Romy smiles at her.

                    ROMY
               (to Esme)
          See?

Robert walks over with a tray full of drinks. Esme gets up.
From a distance Romy watches Samuel, he is telling a joke,
dancing strangely. When Esme rejoins them, she stands close
to him and touches his arm. Briefly Samuel's hand rests on
Esme's back. A wave of jealousy rushes through Romy's body.
Suddenly, the waiter puts a glass of milk down in front of
Romy, snapping her out of her haze. The men and women at her
table laugh and look around, to see who ordered it, but it's
unclear.

                    ROMY (CONT'D)
          Did you order this?

                    TOM
          No...

Romy makes eye contact with Samuel, who watches her from the
bar. She reaches for the glass.

                    HAZEL
               (whispers)
          Are you gonna drink that? Don't
          drink that-

Slowly, Romy drinks the entire glass of milk while making eye
contact with Samuel. Some business men behind her start
laughing.

INT. LUXURIOUS BAR MIDTOWN- NIGHT

LATER- The bar is totally empty. Romy pays the bill. The
group of interns, including Esme, have left. Suddenly Samuel
walks out of the men's room. He doesn't look at Romy but when
he walks past her he whispers in her ear.

                    SAMUEL
          Good girl.

Romy freezes. He keeps on walking to the exit.

INT. OFFICE BUILDING ROMY'S OFFICE- NIGHT

Romy is running late. Laying on the floor, she tries to get
into a huge, beautiful blue dress. She squirms like a snake
shedding its skin. We hear the final scene of Jacob's Hedda
Gabler.

                              HEDDA O.S.
                         (scared)
                    And what will I do in the evenings?

                              TESMAN O.S.
                    Oh I'm sure judge Brack will be
                    more than happy to keep you
                    company.

                              BRACK O.S.
                    Absolutely dear Hedda! We will have
                    a ball!

                              HEDDA O.S.
                         (emotional)
                    Oh yes you would love that,
                    wouldn't you judge Brack?
                         (screams)
                    To be the only cock in my run?

A loud shot is fired. Hedda kills herself. A scream.

                              BRACK O.S.
                    Who does such a thing?

Applause.

                                                      CUT TO:

INT. THEATRE- OPENING NIGHT

The curtains are closed. The last few people walk out. An usher picks up playbills. Romy sits alone in her dress, staring at the empty stage. She looks around, unsure where to go.

INT. THEATRE BACKSTAGE STAIRCASE/HALLWAY- NIGHT

Romy walks down a staircase, looking for the dressing room. An actor with a wig in her hand runs by her, laughing.

INT. THEATRE SCARLETT'S DRESSING ROOM- NIGHT

People are crammed in the small dressing room. Romy walks in. Everyone is drinking, sweating and raving about the show. Adrenaline is high. Her phone buzzes. An older actor, Stephen (the actor who plays BRACK) is imitating a robot. "Bleep, bleep!" Romy observes Jacob.

His almost childlike, happy face makes her smile. Stephen embraces Romy. Her phone keeps buzzing.

      ROMY
     (to Stephen)
  You were wonderful!

Distracted, Romy looks at her phone.

      STEPHEN
  Do you have phone addiction? It's a
  serious issue-

She looks straight into his eyes.

      ROMY
  No, Stephen, I have a job.

She takes his glass of champagne and finishes it.

      STEPHEN
  I thought you didn't drink-

She walks over to Jacob who is talking to Scarlett.

      ROMY
     (genuine)
  It was wonderful, just wonderful!
     (to Scarlett)
  You were amazing- you made me cry.
     (whispers in his ear)
  I have to go. Work emergency.

He grabs her.

JACOB	ROMY (CONT'D)
No.	Sorry.

      JACOB (CONT'D)
     (whispers in her ear)
  It's the one night I need you by my
  side.

ROMY	JACOB (CONT'D)
I know. I'm so sorry. It's just there is so much pressure now-	Come on. You can't go.

Curious, Scarlett looks at Romy.

      SCARLETT
  How are you?

                    ROMY
          I'm sorry. I have to go-

Other people start to notice the tension between the couple.
Romy starts to leave, Jacob follows her into the tiny
hallway. He grabs her arm.

                    JACOB
          Romy!

                    ROMY
            (sweet)
          I really have to go. So sorry. Have
          fun. It was wonderful!

She manages to escape.

INT. OFFICE EXECUTIVE FLOOR HALLWAYS -NIGHT

Cautiously, Romy walks down the hallway in her dress, not
sure what to expect.

INT. OFFICE BUILDING ROMY'S OFFICE -NIGHT

Embarrassed, Romy falls into her chair. On her desk she finds
a note. It has a date, time, and address written on it.

EXT. OFFICE BUILDING - NIGHT

From the street, Samuel looks up at Romy's office windows.
Watching her. He smokes a cigarette.

EXT. 27TH STREET- DUSK

Tense, Romy walks down the street in a designer coat. It's
cold.

INT. CHEAP HOTEL ROOM- NIGHT

Romy enters the worn out room. She looks around. The walls
are painted red. She notices a stain on the carpet.

                    ROMY
          Hello?

She takes her coat off. In a beautiful, expensive outfit, she
sits down on the edge of the bed. She isn't used to waiting
for anything. She finds a long, dark hair on the bed. She
picks it up and studies it.

She takes a cheap piece of strawberry candy wrapped in red paper out of a bowl. Samuel enters with a small plastic bag from a bodega.

                  SAMUEL
               (indifferent)
          Oh. You're here.

He is wearing a hoody and jeans, the hood over his head. He doesn't look at her. Slowly, he takes some items out of the bag. Nervous, she watches him. Tension builds between them.

                  ROMY
          Sit down.

He immediately does.

                  ROMY (CONT'D)
          Your behavior is unacceptable.

                  SAMUEL
               (he smiles)
          What behavior?

                  ROMY
               (convincing herself)
          That's all I have to say and that's
          the only reason I'm here-

                  SAMUEL
          What are you talking about?

He laughs. Amused by her anger.

                  ROMY
          -to stop this and your wild
          behavior.

                  SAMUEL
          What does that mean?

                  ROMY
          Leaving me notes? Calling me?
          Sending me milk?

                  SAMUEL
               (smiles)
          Well- you drank it all...

                  ROMY
          Texting me? Inviting me to this
          ridiculous hotel? Keeping me
          waiting- Are you fucking insane?

He gets up. While she keeps talking he slowly walks towards her.

                    ROMY (CONT'D)
          We need to have a very serious
          conversation, you and I, we need to
          talk this through. Get to the
          bottom of it. You need to realize
          that what you're doing is wrong-

He puts his hand on her mouth.

                    SAMUEL
            (soft)
          I don't think I want to talk.

He grabs the back of her head and pushes her face into the dirty carpet. For a brief moment, he holds her down like a kitten. Quickly, he lets her go. He scares himself, struggling to control his impulses. Both of them are lost for a moment.

                    SAMUEL (CONT'D)
          Sorry but- I'm confused -
          You don't know me. I'm a total-
          stranger, but you show up here,
          dressed like this- and you want me
          to just look at you- and- not do
          anything?

Romy is quiet.

                    SAMUEL (CONT'D)
          I'm not some thing you can just
          pick up and play with.

                    ROMY
            (annoyed)
          Oh, shut the fuck up.

                    SAMUEL
          Get on your knees.

                    ROMY
            (chuckles)
          What? No!

He laughs, embarrassed.

                    SAMUEL
            (smiling)
          I just feel...Is That what you
          want? I don't know how to- If
          that's what you want - Be honest.
                    (MORE)

                    SAMUEL (CONT'D)
               (seriously asking)
          Is it?

                    ROMY
               (honest)
          I don't know.

She looks at him. She shifts her tone.

                    ROMY (CONT'D)
               (quietly, genuine)
          You're very young- I don't want to
          hurt you.

                    SAMUEL
          Hurt me? I think I have power over
          you, not the other way around. I
          mean, one call and you lose
          everything. Right?

With an inquiring look he stares at her, curious what she
will say or do.

                    SAMUEL (CONT'D)
               (whispers)
          Does that turn you on, when I say
          that?

It does but she is too embarrassed to admit it. She sort of
rolls her eyes and shakes her head. He studies her like a
biologist.

                    SAMUEL (CONT'D)
               (whispers, sweetly)
          Get on your knees.

For a moment she tries to bend her knees. Then quickly:

                    ROMY
               (decisive)
          Ok. I have to go.

She walks to the door, he takes a step towards her. She feels
him behind her. Quickly, she turns around and grabs his face
and kisses him passionately. Gently, he pushes her away.

                    SAMUEL
               (genuine)
          No. Not like that. I don't like it
          like that. I don't want it like
          that-

Rejected she attacks him, trying to trigger his aggression.
They land on the floor. They struggle, they wrestle.

She jumps up. He pulls her down and turns her on her belly. While she crawls away from him he takes her leg. He kisses her leg, sniffs it, bites it, and slides her body back to him. She turns towards him, grabs his arm. When she wants to look at him, he covers her eyes.

                    SAMUEL (CONT'D)
          Don't.

The more he tells her not to, the harder she keeps trying to find his gaze. With her fingers she opens his eyes and forces him to look at her. He laughs.

                    SAMUEL (CONT'D)
          Stop! Stop!

She does. Careful, he takes her hand and pulls her up. They walk around the small room hand in hand, as if they are two young lovers, sightseeing on a city trip. He guides her to a corner of the room, he leaves her there, facing the wall. He goes to sit on the bed to catch his breath, to think. A long beat. Calmly, she stands in the corner, waiting.

                    SAMUEL (CONT'D)
          Please take your clothes off-

                    ROMY
          No.

                    SAMUEL
              (soft)
          Why not?

                    ROMY
              (scared to show her body
               to such a young man)
          I don't know. I don't want to.

                    SAMUEL
              (kind)
          Ok. That's ok.

With his hand he gestures for her to come sit next to him on the bed. She does. For a short moment she lays her head on his shoulder.

                    SAMUEL (CONT'D)
          Would you mind getting on your
          hands and knees for me?

                    ROMY
          Why?

He breathes in, trying to calm himself, understand himself, and to slow down. He takes a piece of candy out of the bowl.

> SAMUEL
> (smiling)
> Could you maybe try? For the sake of what we're trying to...do here?

She shakes her head. He waits. He observes her, trying to measure her response. Slowly she gets up and bends her knees. First, she kneels in front of him. She looks at him with questioning eyes. She places both her hands in front of her, on the carpet. When she is on all fours, he holds out his hand. He makes soft, sweet sounds with his mouth as if calling a puppy. Hesitant, she crawls towards him. Ashamed, she eats the candy from his hand. While she chews, he strokes her head. He goes to sit next to her on the floor. He lays her flat on her belly. Gently, he caresses her. His hand slides under her skirt. He starts to pleasure her. She lets it happen. After a while she feels like it's taking too long and tries to get up.

> SAMUEL (CONT'D)
> (kind)
> No- no. It's ok-

He gently holds her down. She closes her eyes. She tries to surrender. He takes his time. She starts to shake a little bit.

> ROMY
> (whispers, embarrassed)
> I'm gonna...I don't wanna pee-

70 He keeps going. Torn between guilt and joy, she breathes in. He feels her very slowly reaching her climax. Her whole body starts to shake. She orgasms for real. An unfamiliar sound escapes her. More growling than moaning. This has never happened to her before. Overwhelmed by her reaction to his touch, he holds her. A wave of emotion washes over her. Embarrassed, she tries to hold back her tears. Calmly, he looks at her vulnerable eyes. Protective, he holds her in his arms. She lets go and cries.

INXS, Never Tear Us Apart, starts play to quietly.

Later- They sit next to each other on the edge of the bed. Samuel is shirtless, Romy wears Samuel's hoodie. He reaches over, and zips up the sweater, then puts the hood over her head.

42.

INT/EXT. MONTAGE - VARIOUS

Never Tear Us Apart continues to play while we see Samuel and Romy's connection deepen in the office and outside of it.

- INT. OFFICE LOBBY: Romy walks past the lit up Christmas tree.

- INT. OFFICE ELEVATOR: Romy is in the elevator, Samuel enters. She blushes. They share a moment before Esme and a group of interns rush in. Suddenly, Romy is surrounded by young people, laughing and talking loudly. Romy watches as Samuel and Esme laugh together, Samuel touches Esme's arm.

- INT. ROMY'S PRIVATE OFFICE

Samuel enters Romy's private office.

                    SAMUEL
          You wanted to see me?

                    ROMY
          Yes, sit down.

She motions for him to sit opposite her.

- INT. ROMY'S PRIVATE OFFICE BATHROOM: Samuel and Romy kiss passionately. He pushes her up against the wall, his hand around her neck.

-INT. OFFICE CONFERENCE ROOM: Romy holds court in a meeting, surrounded by men in suits. She looks up as Samuel walks by.

- INT. OFFICE PRESS ROOM: Romy delivers a speech. She makes eye contact with Samuel through the glass walls.

- INT. ROMY'S PRIVATE OFFICE BATHROOM: Romy enters her bathroom, Samuel is already there peeing in her toilet. She embraces him from behind. He finishes peeing. They kiss passionately. He puts his thumb in her mouth.

- INT. UPSTATE HOUSE BEDROOM: Romy and her whole family sleep together in a big, cozy bed.

- INT. ROMY'S PRIVATE OFFICE BATHROOM: Romy lays face down on the floor, she pulls her dress up over het waist. Samuel gets down on the ground behind her.

- EXT. ALLEYWAY: Samuel kisses Romy against a wall in a dirty alleyway.

- INT. OFFICE KITCHEN: It's late. Romy looks out at the city lights through the window.

- EXT. ALLEYWAY: Samuel turns Romy around, presses her face up against the wall. He covers her eyes and starts to have sex with her from behind.

- INT. OFFICE KITCHEN: Samuel enters. Romy sees him in the reflection of the window. He comes up behind her, and takes a coffee cup form the shelf. To her surprise, he lets it slide out of his hands. The cup breaks into pieces on the floor. He looks at the shards and at her.

                  SAMUEL
           (calm)
      Why don't you clean that up?

Slowly, Romy gets down on her hands and knees. Carefully she gathers the pieces in her hand. She focusses on the task, trying to execute it precisely. With his foot he kicks some of the shards towards her. She lays her head on his shoe.

- EXT. ALLEYWAY: Romy and Samuel kiss, post-coital. Romy caresses Samuel's face. She looks at him with soft, loving eyes. Grateful. We see the lights of the city.

INT. UPSTATE HOUSE- KITCHEN- NIGHT

Full of new found energy Romy prepares a meal. A fire crackles, a beautifully decorated Christmas tree, *classical music is playing*. Perfect happiness. The family is gathered for a cozy dinner. Isabel's girlfriend, Mary, is at the table too. Romy is on top of the world. She is dancing. Jacob enjoys his wife's mood.

                  ISABEL
           (laughing)
      Mom! Stop.

Nora joins her mother and starts to make wild dance moves. Romy goes out of her way to show Mary a good time. Jacob quietly observes his cheerful wife and daughter interacting.

INT. UPSTATE HOUSE- BEDROOM- NIGHT

In the bedroom Romy and Jacob, sit under the bed sheet like two children. They speak in hushed voices about their daughter and her girlfriend. The tone is playful and happy.

                  ROMY
      Did you notice how Isabel set the
      table, and helped with everything?
      She never does that.

JACOB
          They seem so happy together, it's
          wonderful. And Mary...I think she's
          a great girl.

Romy laughs, Jacob studies her face.

INT. UPSTATE HOUSE KITCHEN- NIGHT

Isabel sits on the kitchen counter by the oven, smoking a cigarette. She blows smoke into the range hood. Quietly, Romy walks up to her and sits next to her. Without chastising her, she takes the cigarette and puts it in her own mouth. Surprised, Isabel smiles. Romy is able to be more intimate with her daughter now that something has been unlocked inside of her. She puts her arm around her.

EXT./ INT. UPSTATE HOUSE HALLWAYS/ DINING ROOM-DAY

We follow Romy as she enters the house carrying a fancy shopping bag. While walking, she takes off her coat in front of the mirror. She is wearing a revealing new dress, a stark contrast to her usual work suits. Suddenly she hears Samuel's voice. Shocked, she hides behind the open door and listens.

                    SAMUEL O. S
               (about his father)
          -he was like working for VIP's and
          political leaders and stuff.
          Protecting them. He was a fighter.
          Incredibly strong. Incredibly
          smart. Later he became a
          philosophy teacher. He wrote these
          beautiful poems-

When Romy enters the dining room she sees Samuel at the dining table talking with her family. Tea cups, coffee and cookies on the table. Jacob is taking in every word Samuel says. He is inspired by his story. The girls are very charmed by him. Samuel stops talking when he sees Romy. He holds up her laptop.

                    SAMUEL
               (enthusiastic)
          Hey! You forgot your laptop at the
          office! Esme told me to bring it to
          you!

Romy hides her panic.

                    SAMUEL (CONT'D)
She said you couldn't survive a
minute without it.

                    ROMY
She couldn't send a messenger?

                    SAMUEL
         (smiling)
I thought- better in person- in
case... Sensitive information... I
took the train.

                    JACOB
Is that a new dress? You look hot!

                    ISABEL
Dad! Eeeww-

                    JACOB
What?

                    NORA
         (to Samuel)
Do you work with the robots?

                    SAMUEL
No, not directly! I'm only an
intern, so I have to work very hard
to prove myself first!

                    ISABEL
Do they pay you?

                    SAMUEL
Yes. Of course. And I work at a
bar.

                    ISABEL
What bar?

                    SAMUEL
The Nines.

                    NORA
I am named after a play.

                    SAMUEL
What? A play? Which one?

                    NORA
I'm a dancer. You want to see me
dance the Tarantella?

                              SAMUEL
                    Yes!

Nora starts to dance.

                              ROMY
                         (cold)
                    We have to go soon.

Quickly, Samuel gets up.

                              SAMUEL
                         (blushing)
                    Oh! I'm so sorry. Yes. Of course!

Embarrassed, he smiles. Jacob puts his hand on his arm.

                              JACOB
                    Do you want some more coffee?

Unsure of himself, Samuel looks at Romy. Is he allowed to
stay?

                              SAMUEL
                         (to Nora)
                    You're a great dancer.

                              ISABEL
                    You want to come to come on a hike
                    with us?

Samuel looks at Romy, who tries to hide her panic.

EXT. UPSTATE FOREST BEHIND THEIR HOUSE-DAY

The family are on a hike. Samuel watches as the children run
up behind Jacob and jump on his back, yelling and laughing.
They play wrestle - Samuel reaches out his hand to join in.

From in the distance Romy, looks down at them all having a
good time.

INT. /EXT.   UPSTATE CAR/ PARKING LOT TRAIN STATION- LATE
AFTERNOON

The car is parked. Romy and Samuel sit in silence.

                              SAMUEL
                    They're so nice- You're family-
                    That's what I want, for myself.
                    Later.

Romy turns towards him. Her eyes are dark.

                    ROMY
          Don't ever show up like that again.

                    SAMUEL
          What? I was just- doing my job.

                    ROMY
               (calm but threatening)
          My family is everything to me.
          Don't you ever do that again.

                    SAMUEL
          What are you talking about?

Hurt, he wants to get out of the car but the door is locked.
He tries again. She doesn't open it.

                    SAMUEL (CONT'D)
          Let me out!

          ROMY   SAMUEL (CONT'D)
Listen.   Jesus Christ. Open the door.

                    ROMY (CONT'D)
          Wait.

Realizing she has to manage the situation, she tries to calm
him down. She touches his arm. Even though he is angry and
hurt, her touch relaxes him.

                    ROMY (CONT'D)
          I'm sorry. Lets calm down and talk
          for a moment. I was just- I didn't
          expect you to show up at my house!

She puts his hand on his leg. She looks at him with soft
eyes.

                    ROMY (CONT'D)
          I don't think- We can see each
          other outside of work anymore-

                    SAMUEL
               (with controlled anger)
          Take your hand of my leg.

Quickly she takes it away.

                    ROMY
          Sorry.

A beat. They both think about it. He turns towards her.

SAMUEL
Romy, I don't want a girlfriend, if that's what you're afraid off. You look like a... mother. I'm not- I'm not interested in that.

She looks at him. He tries to explain how he sees it:

SAMUEL (CONT'D)
I thought what we were doing- It's like- In my mind- We're like--two children. Playing. It's natural.

ROMY
(quickly)
You're not a child.

SAMUEL
Whatever.

He tries to open the door.

SAMUEL (CONT'D)
(calm)
Unlock the car. Unlock the car! Or do you want to keep me here?

She doesn't open the door. He raises his voice.

SAMUEL (CONT'D)
(aggressive)
Unlock the fucking car!!
(emotional)
Why are you making me like this? I don't want to feel like this!

Worried, she grabs his arm.

ROMY
Hey!! Listen! This stops here, whatever this is. I'm sorry if it is confusing for you. It's confusing for me too- for the both of us.

She looks at his face, his skin.

ROMY (CONT'D)
You're very... young.

SAMUEL
No- I'm not-

                    ROMY
          You are-
               (she pauses)
          I'm not going to...fire you but we
          have to keep it- professional.

                    SAMUEL
          What the fuck does that mean?

                    ROMY
          I'm just trying to take care of you
          here.

                    SAMUEL
          You're taking care of me?
               (he shakes his head)
          No.

They lock eyes. They know they are in dangerous territory. She unlocks the car. He gets out. She looks at him walking away. She drives off.

INT. AUTOMATED WAREHOUSE- DAY

Overhead shot of a fully automated warehouse. Robots are moving faster and faster, picking and placing products in endless amounts of boxes and containers while *business radio is playing louder and louder.*

INT. ROMY AND JACOB'S APARTMENT- BATHROOM DAY

Business news continues to play. Close on Romy's face as she looks at herself in the mirror. She closes her eyes.

INT. OFFICE BUILDING HALLWAY/ ROMY'S OFFICE- DAY

Romy walks towards her office. Through the glass walls, she sees Samuel talking to Mr. Missel in her office. Nervous, she watches them.

INT. OFFICE BUILDING ROMY'S OFFICE-DAY

Romy walks in, Samuel smiles politely at her.

                    SAMUEL
               (to Mr. Missel)
          Thank you so much!

Samuel leaves. Frightened that Samuel spoke to Mr. Missel about her, she smiles.

                    ROMY
          You were looking for me?

                    MR. MISSEL
          Look at this!

Amused, he shows her the coffee Samuel brought him.

                    MR. MISSEL (CONT'D)
          I didn't even ask for it! Very
          bright kid!

Romy sits down. He looks at her, she forces a smile on her face.

                    MR. MISSEL (CONT'D)
          I wanted to talk to you about the
          tapes Hazel sent over- it's ok to
          relax a little. You don't need to
          be scared of their questions.

                    ROMY
               (submissive)
          Yes, yes, I was a little tense I
          get that-

Romy gets a text. "ROOF".

                    MR MISSEL
               (fatherly, warm)
          No need, no need, you've done it a
          million times before-

                    ROMY
               (looking at her phone)
          Excuse me- Sebastian-I'm going to
          have to take this.

Quickly, she gets up.

EXT. OFFICE BUILDING ROOF DAY

High up, on top of the building, Romy finds Samuel. Smoking a cigaret, he looks out over the city. It's snowing. Cautious, she walks towards him.

                    ROMY
          What's going on? Are you ok?

Samuel is quiet for a moment. He inhales.

                    SAMUEL
          Yeah I'm fine- I just eh- I don't
          feel comfortable working for you
          anymore.

Worried, Romy stares at him.

                    SAMUEL (CONT'D)
          I'm going to talk to someone and
          ask to be transferred to a
          different department.

                    ROMY
               (hiding her panic)
          You can't do that- They will ask
          questions. They will investigate.
          You can't- You can't do that- They
          could- fire me.

                    SAMUEL
          I thought this was your company.

                    ROMY
          That doesn't matter.

He takes a step towards her. He tries to suppress his
emotions, his fear, tries to ignore her vulnerable eyes. He
swallows.

                    SAMUEL
          It's for the best. For both of us.

He walks away. Romy panics.

                    ROMY
               (terrified)
          Wait! Samuel! Wait! Wait!

He is gone. For a brief moment Romy looks at the edge of the
roof as if it invites her to come closer.

INT. ROMY AND JACOB'S APARTMENT- BEDROOM- NIGHT

In bed, Romy is glued her phone, waiting for Samuel to call
or text. Sensing her distance, Jacob tries to initiate sex.
He wants to comfort and kiss her, to make love to her.

                    JACOB
          You want to play a little bit?

                    ROMY
               (lying)
          Yeah-

She tries to open up to him, smile, kiss him back, but she can't. His touch, his scent, his breath, make her angry. Aggressively, she rejects him. When he doesn't back off, she pushes him away. Hard. Hurt, he looks at her.

>   JACOB
>   (startled)
>   Why did you do that?

She studies his face, a flood of mixed emotions. Frustration builds up inside her.

>   ROMY
>   (quietly, emotional)
>   I've never had an orgasm with you-

>   JACOB
>   What?

He reaches for her arm.

>   ROMY
>   (hisses)
>   Don't fucking touch me-

She turns her back to him, tears in her eyes.

>   ROMY (CONT'D)
>   I can't- I can't come with you.

>   JACOB
>   Are you alright? Hey-

>   ROMY
>   No-

She gets out of bed, grabs her phone, and walks out.

EXT. STREETS OF NEW YORK- NIGHT

In the middle of the night she walks through the dark streets of the city. She is wearing Ugg boots. A coat over her nightgown.

INT. THE NINES BAR- NIGHT.

Cautiously, Romy walks in. Samuel is working behind the quiet bar. He looks like a prince in his tuxedo. Enthusiastically, he is telling two beautiful older women a story. Surprised to see Romy he looks up. When she tries to greet him, he ignores her. He whispers something in his COLLEAGUE'S(JOSH, 24) ear. Josh walks up to her.

                          JOSH
                    (whispers)
               I think it's time to leave-

                          ROMY
                    (whispers back)
               Leave? Why? I need to talk to him.

                          JOSH
               I'm sorry- but he says you need to
               leave-

                          ROMY
                    (humiliated)
               He said that?

                          JOSH
               Yes... Right now.

She looks at Samuel who looks away. Elegantly, Josh helps her
up. He escorts Romy to the door. Before she exits, Samuel
looks at her.

INT. ROMY AND JACOB'S APARTMENT- KITCHEN DAY

In the early morning, Romy and Jacob stand in the kitchen. A
tense silence between them. Jacob is on his way out but
lingers.

                          JACOB
               Did you order the headphones for
               Isabel's birthday?

She nods. She stares at the gifts. He is waiting for her to
start talking. She doesn't.

                          JACOB (CONT'D)
                    (with controlled
                     frustration)
               Did you- Did you mean what you
               said? About never-

                          ROMY
                    (emotional)
               I was just taking it out on you- Of
               course I didn't mean it. That would
               be- Nineteen years of- I mean; no,
               I was angry. I was stressed. Of
               course I didn't mean it- I am
               sorry.

                    JACOB
               (vulnerable)
          I- I've never- Normally, you know-
          Women- you know, they-

                    ROMY
          I'm not normal. I'm not other
          women! Look at me. I'm not normal.

She wants him to comfort her. He stares at her.

                    JACOB
               (to hurt her)
          No. You're not.

He walks out.

INT. OFFICE BUILDING WINDOWLESS BASEMENT ROOM- DAY

Romy sits at the small table. Her hair is messy. Her palms
are sweaty. Anxious, she stares at the door. Her heart is
beating too fast. She lays her hand on her chest to calm
herself down. After a while, Samuel enters. Quickly, she gets
up.

                    ROMY
          Hi-

                    SAMUEL
          I have 7 minutes.

                    ROMY
          Thank you for coming.

He leans against a wall. He remains silent. Her mind is
racing.

                    ROMY (CONT'D)
               (worried)
          Did you talk to them already?

He doesn't respond. She tries to sound calm. In charge.

                    ROMY (CONT'D)
          Ok. So. What can we do to- solve
          this? To make you feel better?

                    SAMUEL
          You're sweating.

Embarrassed, she touches her forehead.

ROMY
Sorry.

A long beat. He thinks.

SAMUEL
(genuine)
Do you want to lose everything?

ROMY
What?

SAMUEL
You give that impression.

ROMY
What do you mean?

SAMUEL
The way you look at me.
As if you're expecting me to- do that. To take it all away.

She shakes her head.

ROMY
No.

SAMUEL
Until you have nothing? Until you are nothing?

SAMUEL (CONT'D)
Are you using me to do that?

ROMY
(convincing herself)
No, of course not.

SAMUEL
That scares the shit out of me.

ROMY
(firm)
No- I'm not doing that. I promise. I'm not.
(speaking slowly to convince him)
I just think cause you're young and I'm older than you-
(searching for the right words)
I want to be protective. I don't want to hurt you-

                    SAMUEL
          You keep saying that- but- I'm
          fine. I'm totally fine. I think
          you're the one who's hurting.

A beat. His words touch her. She feels seen. He shifts his
tone. Her vulnerability softens his heart. He goes to sit
down.

                    SAMUEL (CONT'D)
               (reassuring)
          Listen- You don't have to worry
          about it. What we do is- If we
          continue to do this-
               (fatherly, explaining)
          It's totally normal. I mean... - as
          long as it's... you know-
          consensual-

                    ROMY
               (cold)
          What does that mean?

                    SAMUEL
          It's about giving and taking power,
          no?

                    ROMY
               (sarcastic)
          Come on- What did you do? Go to the
          library, looked it up?

                    SAMUEL
          No! I'm just saying- It has nothing
          to do with your- family or the
          company- It's between us.

                    ROMY
          I'm sorry. I didn't mean to- I'm
          just nervous.

                    SAMUEL
          You're nervous? Yeah you look
          nervous. You're all.. You're acting
          all...

He imitates her nervous gestures.

                    SAMUEL (CONT'D)
               (genuine)
          Why are you nervous? Why are you so
          nervous?

She shrugs, a faint smile in her eyes.

                    SAMUEL (CONT'D)
          Just to be safe- If we continue to
          do this- We need to set some rules-
          that you and I both agree on. Like;
          I don't know....
                  (as if he is making it up
                   as he goes)
          ...starting with: I tell you what
          to do and- you do it.

He smiles, aware of how that sounds.

                    ROMY
          Oh, come on... Jesus Christ!

Samuel gets up to leave.

                    SAMUEL
              (rejected)
          See! This is what I mean- this is
          what I'm talking about-

He walks to the door. Worried, Romy tries to stop him from
leaving.

                    ROMY
          I'm sorry, I'm so sorry, No, no,
          no, wait come on- Sit down. I'm
          sorry- Sit down.

He hesitates.

                    ROMY (CONT'D)
          Please?

He sits back down again. They look at each other. Silence.
Tension builds. He is waiting for her to speak.

                    SAMUEL
          You have to be the one to say it.
          That's how this works.

                    ROMY
          How what works? I don't-

                    SAMUEL
          This! The dynamic. It's about
          trust!

                    ROMY
              (half smiling)
          I thought you said it had to be
          consensual.

He can't help but laugh.

						SAMUEL
				Yes, that's what consent is Romy!
				That's what it is. You have to
				agree to it. Both parties have to
				agree to it.

						ROMY
				And if I don't?

						SAMUEL
				Then I will have to go talk to
				someone-

						ROMY
				No, don't do that. Please?

They look at each other.

						SAMUEL
					(genuine)
				Come on. Just admit that this is
				what you want. Be honest.

She exhales, nervous. He studies her.

						SAMUEL (CONT'D)
				You don't look comfortable. You
				don't look comfortable at all-
					(he pauses)
				Why don't you sit over there?

He points to the table.

						SAMUEL (CONT'D)
				Sit on the edge, right there-

She stares at him. Slowly, she gets up and walks over to the edge of the table. She sits down and looks at him unsure of what he expects her to do. He gets up and pretends to move to the door.

						SAMUEL (CONT'D)
				Ok, you need to say it out loud,
				otherwise I'm gonna have to go talk
				to someone and ask to be
				transferred-

			ROMY						SAMUEL (CONT'D)
	No, wait wait-					I'll go talk to them-

                    ROMY (CONT'D)
               (as if asking for a line)
          What are the words?

                    SAMUEL
               (smiling at her childlike
                behavior)
          You know the words.

                    ROMY
          I don't- I- don't.

                    SAMUEL
               (a little exasperated)
          You do. Just say it.

                    ROMY
          Ok, ok--I'll say it.

He steps towards her, places his hand on her thigh. She
inhales deeply. He whispers into her ear:

                    SAMUEL
          I need to hear you say...

He slides his hand under her skirt. She can't help but moan.

                    SAMUEL (CONT'D)
          You can do it.

                    ROMY
               (whispering)
          What do you want me to say?

                    SAMUEL
               (slowly)
          I... will... do...

                    ROMY
          I will do-

She feels his fingers between her legs.

                    SAMUEL
          Whatever you tell me to do.

                    ROMY
          Whatever you tell me to do.

His scent makes her brain melt. She starts to breath heavily.

                    ROMY (CONT'D)
          I will do whatever you tell me to
          do.

                    SAMUEL
          Say it again.

She looks up at him like a child.

                    ROMY
          I will do whatever you tell me to
          do.

                    SAMUEL
          Good.

Quickly, he pulls his hand out from her skirt, and walks out
the room. Leaving her on edge. Her eyes go dark. She is
panting.

INT. LUXURIOUS HOTEL ROOM DAY

The presidential suite. A long hallway with doors leading to
the many different beautiful, luxurious rooms. Romy stands in
front of a golden mirror and checks her reflection. A knock
on the door. She starts walking towards it.

INT. LUXURIOUS HOTEL- SUITE- DAY

1. Nervous, Romy opens the door. They both smile. He walks
past her.

                    SAMUEL
               (childlike)
          Hey! There's a whole living room in
          here!

2. Cut to: Silence. Totally different atmosphere. Romy sits
on a sofa in the living room. He sits opposite her. She wants
to get up and kiss him.

                    SAMUEL (CONT'D)
          Stay.

She sits down. He stares at her.

                    ROMY
          Don't stare at me.

                    SAMUEL
          Why?

                    ROMY
          I don't like to be looked at.

                    SAMUEL
          Ok.
              (he looks away)
          I understand that.
              (a beat)
          Go make yourself a drink.

                    ROMY
          I don't- (drink).

She stops herself. Gets up, and takes one of the small
bottles of liquor. She sits down again. She takes a small
sip.

                    SAMUEL
          All of it.

                    ROMY
          No.

                    SAMUEL
              (smiling)
          Don't say no.

She drinks.

                    SAMUEL (CONT'D)
          Take your panties off.

She looks at her hands.

                    ROMY
          You take them off.

                    SAMUEL
              (calmly smiling)
          Don't tell me what to do.

She takes them off.

                    SAMUEL (CONT'D)
          Open your legs.

She does. A tiny bit. He looks at her.

                    SAMUEL (CONT'D)
          How does that make you feel?

                    ROMY
          Scared.

                    SAMUEL
          Ok.
               (he pauses)
          You want to take your dress off for
          me now? So I can see you?

She shakes her head.

                    SAMUEL (CONT'D)
          But you're going to do it anyway?

She pauses, thinks about it for a moment and nods.

                    SAMUEL (CONT'D)
          -can't hear you-

                    ROMY
          Yes.

                    SAMUEL
          Yes what?

                    ROMY
          Yes, I will take my dress off.

                    SAMUEL
          Ok.

She gets up. She turns around and starts to unzip the dress.
When it falls to the floor, she takes her bra off, still with
her back to him. Slowly, unsure of herself, she turns towards
him. With her hands she tries to cover herself. He studies
her body, taking his time to admire it. She blushes.

                    SAMUEL (CONT'D)
          You're beautiful.

Embarrassed, she looks away. Standing in front of him like
this makes her feel small. She can't help but get emotional.

                    ROMY
               (soft)
          No...

                    SAMUEL
               (gentle)
          You are.

She shakes her head. Tears in her eyes. All she feels is self
hate. He gets up and gently kisses her, still fully clothed.
She is completely naked, vulnerable. He takes her in his
strong arms. She relaxes.

                    SAMUEL (CONT'D)
          You're so beautiful.

She breathes out.

                    SAMUEL (CONT'D)
               (whispering, almost
                inaudible in her ear)
          You're my babygirl.

Slowly, he guides her down to her knees. She looks up.

                    SAMUEL (CONT'D)
          Go ahead.

She unbuckles his belt. *Father Figure by George Michael starts to play.*

                                                  CUT TO:

3. *While we continue to hear Father Figure over the rest of the scene,* Samuel, a whiskey in his hand, dances shirtless. Across the room, Romy sits in an arm chair watching him, legs crossed in front of her, dressed in a white robe. He dances for her.

4. Cut to: Close on Romy's lips. He sticks his fingers in her mouth. She sucks on them. He moves them in and out of her mouth. They kiss.

5. He dances, she touches his chest. He takes her hand and pulls her close. They slow dance together.

6. Cut to: They sit in the window, very close.

                    SAMUEL (CONT'D)
          What's the safe word?

                    ROMY
          What?

                    SAMUEL
          Don't we need a safe word?

She nods.

                    ROMY
               (shy)
          Eh- Jacob?

                    SAMUEL
               (smiling)
          You're husbands name?

She nods.

                    SAMUEL (CONT'D)
               (kind)
          Ok.

Cut to:

7. They sit on chairs next to each other. A tray filled with cakes and tea between them. He takes a jug of milk and pours some of it into a saucer. He puts it on the floor, between his legs. Patiently, he waits for her to understand what she is supposed to do. She gets down on her hands and knees and crawls to the saucer. When she starts to drink from the milk like a kitten, he gently pulls her hair back. When the saucer is empty, she looks at him, milk dripping off her chin. He kisses her cheeks, her lips. Licks the milk off of her face and lips. They kiss.

8. He carries her in his arms like a baby and moves to the music (*still Father Figure*).

9. Samuel's hand around Romy's throat. He dances with her from behind. As he squeezes her neck, she leans back into his body.

10. In the bedroom they have sex. Romy straddles Samuel as they make love. *Father Figure ends.*

11. They lay under the white sheets, in bed, happily exhausted. Their faces very close together, they look into each others eyes and whisper.

                    SAMUEL (CONT'D)
          Can you do your therapy on me?

                    ROMY
               (laughing)
          No.

                    SAMUEL
          Cause you're afraid of what might
          come out of me?

                    ROMY
          No, because I'm not a therapist.

                    SAMUEL
               (genuine question)
          Do you think I'm a - bad...person?

                    ROMY
          No. You're a lovely person. You
          sense things- You know things- what
          people want- what they need-

                    SAMUEL
          I scare myself. Sometimes.

She moves closer to him.

                    ROMY
          You don't scare me.

She thinks for a moment.

                    ROMY (CONT'D)
          What star sign are you?

He laughs.

                    SAMUEL
          I don't believe in that shit.
              (a beat, he looks into her
               eyes, and then
               vulnerable:)
          Can you hold me?

She does.

INT. JACOB AND ROMY'S APARTMENT LIVING ROOM-DAY

Overhead shot of Nora spinning in her red dress. *Loud music is playing.* She is dancing the tarantella. Nora dances wildly. Beautiful. Animalistic. Out of control. Romy sits on the sofa and stares at her daughter.

INT. EMDR CLINIC/ UNDEFINED SPACE

Romy with headphones and wrist bands on. Her eyes move from left to right, following the light bar. The therapist counts out loud. Flashback to Romy's childhood: kids covered in paint are dancing, screaming-

                                        CUT TO:

INT. ROMY AND JACOB'S APARTMENT- LIVING ROOM- DAY

Teenagers dancing just as wild as Romy did when she was a child. Isabel is turning 16.

Isabel's friends are having fun, among them, Mary. Romy watches them. When the doorbell rings, Romy rushes to the door. She opens the door and is shocked to see Samuel and Esme smiling at her. Esme has a big present in her hands.

              ESME
Hi!

              SAMUEL
Hi!

              ROMY
       (smiling)
Come in!

Hiding her panic, Romy guides them to the living room.

              ESME
       (quiet in her ear, re
        Samuel)
You don't mind, do you?

              ROMY
       (smiling)
No, of course not.

Esme and Samuel greet Isabel.

INT. ROMY AND JACOBS APARTMENT LIVING ROOM-DAY

Worried, Romy observes Samuel who is talking to Jacob. Esme is dancing with Isabel and Mary. She takes out her phone and types. She watches Samuel take out his phone.

INT. ROMY AND JACOB'S APARTMENT- KITCHEN- DAY

Romy is doing the dishes. Samuel enters.

              ROMY
       (whispers)
What are you doing?

              SAMUEL
What do you mean?

              ROMY
Why are you here?
       (she tries to understand)
With her?

              SAMUEL
We see each other.

                    ROMY
          What does that mean?

                    SAMUEL
          What did you want me to say to her?
          'No I can't come with you because-'

                    ROMY
          Are you dating her?

                    SAMUEL
          Isn't that man in the living room
          your husband?

Romy takes a step towards him. With her forehead she touches his, as if she's going to head-butt him. It's intimidating. He pushes back.

                    ROMY
               (whispers)
          I don't want you to see other
          women. You're mine-

Fueled by jealousy she can't control herself. Suddenly, they hear someone coming. When Esme appears in the doorway, Romy drops a glass. Samuel immediately kneels and starts to pick up the shards. Uneasy, Esme stares at them.

                    ESME
          Everything ok?

                    SAMUEL
          I was just asking if I could help
          with anything...

                    ROMY
               (to Samuel)
          Yes!
               (gesturing to the broken
                glass)
          Please, can you clean that up?

Esme isn't sure what is going on. She forces a smile on her face.

                    ESME
          It's a lovely party.

INT. OFFICE BUILDING ROMY'S OFFICE- DAY

Romy stands at the window, she looks down on the city. Esme knocks on the door.

                    ROMY
          Come in.

                    ESME
          You wanted to see me?

                    ROMY
          Yes! Hi! Sit down.

Romy's eyes are soft, her tone friendly.

                    ROMY (CONT'D)
          How are you?

                    ESME
          Well. Thank you. You?

                    ROMY
          How is Samuel?

                    ESME
              (shy)
          What? I thought we were going to
          talk about-

                    ROMY
              (friendly)
          I just wanted to make sure
          everything is ok, since we're
          supposed to discuss your future
          soon-

                    ESME
          Yes. I know. I mean, that's what I-

Romy lowers her voice.

                    ROMY
          You have to be careful, Esme, he's
          an intern.

Romy stops herself. With big eyes, Esme looks at her.

                    ROMY (CONT'D)
          I don't want to sound dramatic, but
          you're in a position of power over
          him.

Esme stares at Romy, with a mixture of suspicion and worry.

                        ESME
                (trying to find the right
                 words)
            Oh- Ehh- we've just been hanging
            out-
                    (fast)
            As friends. We're not-

                        ROMY
            You can tell me anything. You know
            that, right?

                        ESME
            I didn't think it would be a big
            deal to bring him- but you're
            right. I am so sorry-

                        ROMY
            I just want to protect you.

Romy's phone buzzes. Close on the screen: It's Samuel. Like a junky she grabs the phone.

                        ROMY (CONT'D)
            Sorry, one moment-

Quickly, Romy walks out.

                        SAMUEL
                (on the phone)
            I want to see you tonight

Loud House music starts playing.

EXT./ INT. CITY STREETS/ HIGHWAY- UBER BLACK CAR NIGHT

Romy looks out of the window while the car drives out of the city. She watches the Christmas decorations transition into the highway. As the car drives through a deserted area, Romy speaks to Jacob on the phone. *The house music continues to play.* The lyrics of the song seem to be in dialogue with Romy's voice.

                        ROMY
            I have to stay late tonight...don't
            Wait up...
            Yeah I know- Sorry- Don't wait
            for me... Oh and don't forget
            Isabel has soccer tomorrow early
            morning- And Nora has dance- Yeah,
            I'll wake her up... OK... I'll just
            sneak in... Love you.

EXT. WAREHOUSE RAVE- NIGHT

The Uber drops Romy in the abandoned parking lot. Hesitant she gets out of the car. The music is loud and fast. Young people are smoking cigarettes outside. A boy stares at her. For a moment, Romy wants to turn around but the car is gone. She decides to go inside.

INT. WAREHOUSE RAVE - NIGHT

Romy walks through an L shaped tunnel. She passes some young people laughing. She enters a very narrow dark stone corridor. A young man on drugs sticks his tongue out. Trying to find her way to the dance floor. She looks around. Some people are trying to dance with her. The average age is 23. She feels completely out of place in every way. Most of the ravers are shirtless. They move aggressively and violently to the music. Romy is forced to move with them. The sensation of warm, sticky bodies against hers and the dancing reminds her of her childhood. Frightened to fall down and get stepped on, she tries to hold on to sweaty arms and slippery shoulders. People try to dance with her but she pushes them away. All she wants is to find Samuel.

When she finally sees him, he is wildly dancing. His hand on the skull of the boy he is dancing with and the boy's hand on his, a beautiful young girl is dancing close by. When he notices Romy, he smiles enthusiastically and waves. Romy tries to get closer to him, but she isn't able to move, she is wedged between bodies. Samuel is very close to the beautiful girl now. Gasping for air, Romy suppresses a panic attack. Samuel is shouting things at her, but she can't hear him, she is drowning in young flesh. Suddenly, two hands grab her and hold her head up, like a rescue swimmer. The hands belong to a tall muscular woman, she presses Romy's body against hers. Leaning into her, Romy dares to relax a little. The woman kisses her, Romy kisses her back for a brief moment. Someone lets her drink from a bottle of water. Slowly they start to dance. Others join. Faster and faster they move. Samuel makes his way to the group and joins them. Samuel's wet, naked upper body is pushed against Romy's. Happy, Romy wraps her arms around him. The weird, staccato movements of the *Gabber* dance, make Romy laugh. Someone tries to take Romy's jacket off, she lets it happen. Samuel is close to her. Surprised by her risky behavior in public, he observes her. The bodies that seemed to want to crush her moments before, now give her comfort and a sense of belonging. As long as she is with him, glued to him, she can breath. She dances as if her life depends on it. Only for him, she is wild and free. Suddenly he grabs her hand and starts to make his way out of the crowd.

INT. WAREHOUSE LABYRINTH STAIRCASES/ HALLWAYS- NIGHT

Samuel drags Romy through a labyrinth of hallways. He has her hand firmly in his, she almost trips. Both their pupils are big.

INT. WAREHOUSE SMALL ABANDONED ROOM - NIGHT

He leads her into a small worn out space. He sits on the floor and pulls her down too. We hear the house music in the distance. He lights a joint.

          SAMUEL
You know that a cuckoo bird lays eggs in the nest of other birds?

          ROMY
      (laughing)
What?

          SAMUEL
The cuckoo chicks basically grow up in the wrong nest and create chaos-

          ROMY
You're not a bird.

          SAMUEL
      (laughing)
I am.

He looks at her. She brings her face close to his. She whispers in his ear.

          ROMY
      (shy, about Esme)
Do you do with her- what you do with me?

          SAMUEL
      (genuine, sweet)
She's not like that Romy. That's why I like her in a different way. That's why I like myself in a different way, with her.

Her heart hurts. Her eyes tear up. He touches her forehead with his. He kisses her softly, tenderly. She smiles.

INT. ROMY AND JACOB'S APARTMENT- KITCHEN- NIGHT

As quiet as she can, Romy walks into the dark living room, her hair a mess. Startled, Romy stares at Isabel, who sits on the sofa. Romy looks like a creature from the wild.

ROMY
Oh! You're still up.

Romy goes and sits down next to Isabel.

ISABEL
(warm)
I'm worried about you-

ROMY
I- am fine. I was very busy- the past months. It's done. We accomplished a lot.

ISABEL
Are you ok?

ROMY
Yes. Are you okay? How is Mary?

ISABEL
(shyly)
She's good.

Isabel tears up.

ROMY
Bedtime?

Isabel nods.

INT. ROMY AND JACOB'S APARTMENT- KITCHEN DAY

Trying to hide her anxiety, Romy is making pancakes for breakfast. *Classical music playing.* Everyone is rushing to get out of the door on time. Nora in a raincoat and her dance costume, Isabel, wearing a soccer outfit, keeps a close eye on her mother, who is trying to keep it together. A knock at the door, everyone looks up. Romy rushes to answer, but Jacob is already there.

JACOB
Yes?

ROMY
Who is it?

                    JACOB
        Esme.

Esme enters, soaking wet from the rain. She stares at the
perfect family, who stares back at her. Jacob starts to push
the kids toward the door, while putting on his rain coat.

INT. ROMY AND JACOB'S APARTMENT-KITCHEN- DAY

Alone, Esme hugs Romy. Long. In her wet coat, Esme sits on
the white, expensive sofa. She looks at the photos on the
wall of Romy and Jacob with famous actors and political
figures. Nervous, Romy stares at her.

                    ESME
        I genuinely thought women with
        power would behave differently than
        men with power.

                    ROMY
        What makes you say that?

                    ESME
        I tried to speak to you so many
        times about my future at the
        company.

                    ROMY
        I know. I'm sorry. We can discuss
        it now. We all went through- a hard
        time, but it paid off. You were
        part of that, Esme. Part of the
        team who made it happen.

                    ESME
        I don't want you to make any
        promises because you're afraid of
        me.

Confused Romy tries to understand what Esme is trying to say.

                    ROMY
              (genuine)
        I'm not afraid of you.

                    ESME
        I know what's going on between you
        and Samuel.

Romy freezes.

                    ESME (CONT'D)
          I only want what I deserve, not
          what is given to me, to silence me.
          That's how it might have worked
          when you were young, but luckily,
          those days are behind us now.

                    ROMY
          I don't know what you're talking
          about.

                    ESME
          You will never see Samuel again.
          You will be a good leader and you
          will create more opportunities for
          women within the company, and be a
          good example and role model to us
          all.

The two woman look at each other. Romy realizes that Esme
might ruin her life and for a brief moment, that thought
seems strangely liberating.

                    ROMY
          You're confusing ambition with
          morality, those are very different
          things.

                    ESME
          I have no interest in taking you
          down. You are one of the few women
          who made it to the top, my interest
          is to keep you there. But not like
          you are now... As a version of you
          that I can look up to and respect.

Tears in Romy's eyes. Ashamed, she nods her head. Esme
leaves.

INT. ROMY AND JACOB'S APARTMENT- LIVING ROOM- DAY

Later- Romy sits on the sofa in the living room, waiting.
Jacob walks in. She doesn't dare to look at him. She takes a
sip of water.

                    JACOB
          What's going on? Are you ok?

Anxious, with his coat still on, he sits down.

                    ROMY
          I need to -

                    JACOB
          Ok.

A long beat. Her confession comes from very deep within.

                    ROMY
          I- Since I was very little, since I
          can remember even, I've always had
          these specific thoughts-

                    JACOB
          What thoughts?

                    ROMY
          Dark, dark thoughts-

She tries to find the right way to say it.

                    ROMY (CONT'D)
          Thoughts of -- violence. Revolting
          thoughts. Embarrassing.
                (she has a hard time
                 saying the words out
                 loud)
          Of being -forced and hurt, and
          humiliated-

Worried where she is going, Jacob looks at her.

                    ROMY (CONT'D)
          I was so ashamed- I still am. I
          have no idea where they come from,
          who planted them in my brain. I
          would give anything to erase them,
          to delete them-

She forces herself to look at Jacob.

                    ROMY (CONT'D)
          I see myself as a strong, smart
          woman, who is...in control of
          things, who knows what she's doing-
          Who is loving and caring and
          responsible, and who wants to work
          on herself. Not some kind of
          embarrassing-- masochist, or
          ignorant... weak anti feminist who-

                    JACOB
          What are you trying to say? I don't
          understand.

                    ROMY
          I thought it was all connected to
          my childhood- So I tried to work
          through that. Every form of therapy-
          You know that. But it didn't help.
          It doesn't help. I was born with
          it.

                    JACOB
          What do you mean?

                    ROMY
          And I asked , my first -real
          boyfriend, Justin, if he could-
          you know- treat me that way, do
          something to me- but it disgusted
          him- he said. He thought it was
          cliche- Which it is!
               (she pauses, looks at him)
          And with us-

She stops herself. They stare at each other for a beat.

                    ROMY (CONT'D)
               (vulnerable)
          I sometimes- tried to- But you
          never seem to be... into it.

                    JACOB
          Into what exactly?

She can't explain.

                    ROMY
               (from deep within)
          I just want to be normal. I want to
          be normal- I want to be what you
          like. I want to be the woman you
          like-

                    JACOB
               (kind)
          I'm sorry, Romy, I don't know what
          you mean- could you...be a little
          more specific-

                    ROMY
          What I'm saying is: I've never
          experienced any of them. Any of the-
          fantasies. In real life, until-

She holds her breath. He holds his.

ROMY (CONT'D)
I met-

She summons her courage.

JACOB
Until you met- ?

She stops talking, she freezes. His eyes go dark.

JACOB (CONT'D)
(slow and controlled)
Who? Who did you meet?

She can't say it.

ROMY
(whispers)
Ehh- I-

JACOB
Jesus. What happened?

She opens her mouth. Nothing comes out. She can't bring herself to say his name. He speaks quietly.

JACOB (CONT'D)
What? Say something! Jesus Christ! Do I know him?
(he feels sick)
Is it- is it Sebastian?

ROMY
What? No. No!

JACOB
Who?

ROMY (CONT'D)
No-

JACOB (CONT'D)
What did you do? What?

ROMY
No- it- It was a man- A stranger-

JACOB
A stranger?

Romy flushes red.

ROMY
Somehow- he knew. He sensed-

JACOB
What?

ROMY
He knew.

JACOB
What? He knew fucking what?

ROMY
How to be- fearless- around me- or-
I mean-
(trying to find words that
wont hurt)
And I couldn't resist that.

He tries to stay calm.

JACOB
How many times?

ROMY
Once. Only once.

JACOB
Who is this guy? Are you in love
with him?

ROMY
It was as if some sort of animal
woke up inside me.

He stares at her.

ROMY (CONT'D)
(trying to explain
honestly)
For me it's not about a safe space
and a safe word and consent and
"the kink"- I hate that word.

JACOB
(horrified but calm)
Tell me what happened. Just tell
me.

She thinks. She wants to confess her deepest secrets.

ROMY
(genuine)
It has to be- There has to be a
form of actual danger- Something
needs to be at stake. For real.
(she looks at him)
I know, it's gross, it's obscene-
It's a monster- that will destroy-
anything to get-

JACOB
(trying to understand)
So? What did you do? What did he do to you?

ROMY (CONT'D)
(firm)
It's over now. It was like an exorcism, and it's done. It's out of my system. It happened once.

ROMY (CONT'D)
(decisive)
I don't need it anymore. It's done.

A beat. He looks out of the window, trying to process what is happening. Anxious, she continues:

ROMY (CONT'D)
My childhood didn't help. The radical beliefs of my parents. The communes- the lack of boundaries-

JACOB
(controlled aggression)
Oh! You see yourself as a victim? Your blaming this on your childhood?

ROMY
No. Of course not. It's not that-, It's not an excuse. I was born with it.

He is breathing loudly.

ROMY (CONT'D)
(slowly and decisive)
I will never see him again. It happened once. I don't even know his name.

JACOB
(calm)
I want you to leave. Now.

ROMY (CONT'D)
It has nothing to do with us. With the -real- me. With our family. I love you! Please- I'm over it. It's out of me, out of my system.

JACOB (CONT'D)
What are you saying?

ROMY (CONT'D)
I love you. Only you. Please.

JACOB (CONT'D)
(emotional)
It has everything to do with you! There is no excuse for this! Not your mom, not your childhood! You fucking lied to me! To us!
(MORE)

79.

JACOB (CONT'D)
Something needs to be at stake?? I
don't give a shit about your
pathetic, banal sexual fantasies.
It's not about that! You
jeopardized the most important
thing... your children! You make me
sick. Get the fuck out of my house!
Now.

Jacob storms out. Ashamed, Romy stays behind.

EXT. COUNTRY ROADS- NIGHT

From above we see Romy's car make it's way to their upstate house.

EXT. UPSTATE HOUSE- NIGHT

A slow push in on the exterior of the house. Lights behind the windows.

INT. UPSTATE HOUSE LIVING ROOM NIGHT

In the living room, Romy sits in the dark with her coat on, next to the Christmas tree. She is smokes cigarette.

INT. UPSTATE HOUSE BEDROOM- NIGHT

Later: Romy sleeps in bed. She wears a nightgown over her underwear. A sound wakes her up. Frightened, she gets up and walks to the window. To her surprise she sees Samuel swimming in the pool. Steam is rising off of the heated water.

EXT. UPSTATE HOUSE SWIMMING POOL-NIGHT

She walks up to the pool. Samuel keeps swimming.

ROMY
You have to leave. You have to go!

He reaches out his hand, as if he wants her to help him out of the pool, but he pulls her towards him and drags her into the water. For a moment it almost seems as if he wants to drown her. Then he folds his body around hers. Gently he kisses her.

SAMUEL
I could drown you, right here. No one would know it was me.

ROMY
          You should.

They kiss.

INT. UPSTATE HOUSE STUDY/ HALLWAY/ LIVING ROOM -NIGHT

At the fireplace Samuel and Romy sit wrapped in thick blankets, opposite each other. With her finger she moves back and forward in front of his face (her version of EMDR). He follows her finger with his eyes. He smiles.

                    ROMY
          5,4,3,2,1...

He closes his eyes.

                    ROMY (CONT'D)
          How does it feel? What do you see?

He doesn't answer. His cheeks turn red. His eyes twitch.

                    ROMY (CONT'D)
          What does it smell like?

He starts to breathe heavy. A tear rolls down his face. He looks like he is in pain. Romy takes his face in her hands.

                    ROMY (CONT'D)
              (soft)
          Hey, come back to me. Hey-

Slowly, he opens his eyes.

                    ROMY (CONT'D)
          Are you ok?

She looks into his eyes.

                    ROMY (CONT'D)
          What did you see?

He wipes his face. He avoids her gaze.

                    SAMUEL
          You. I saw you.

After a moment of silence, Romy changes the subject:

                    ROMY
          Did I mess with your head?

He thinks about it.

                    SMANUEL
          Yes, you did. But so did I- with
          yours.

She shakes her head.

                    SAMUEL
          We're equally responsible.

                    ROMY
               (decisive)
          No. That doesn't make it okay.

They hear a sound. They look up and to their shock, they see
Jacob. Seemingly calm he looks back at them. No one speaks.
Slowly Samuel and Romy get up. A long beat.

                    JACOB
               (Calm, to his wife)
          Please, give us a minute- Just
          leave us alone.

She doesn't move.

                    JACOB (CONT'D)
          Come on, Romy. Come on- Just give
          me some time with him.

                    ROMY
          No. Jacob- Lets stay calm.

Jacob takes her arm and tries to lead her out of the room but
Romy physically resists. When Jacob starts to push her out,
Samuel lays his hand on Jacob's shoulder, which triggers
Jacob to immediately attack him.

                    ROMY (CONT'D)
          Jacob! No!

The men start to fight. Samuel tries to deescalate, but to no
avail. Romy grabs her husband's arms to make him stop. He
swiftly turns to her and pushes her out of the way.

                    JACOB
               (to Romy)
          Stay back!

Seeing him push Romy, Samuel attacks Jacob. Romy tries to
pull Samuel away from her husband. They destroy a chair; they
drag each other over the expensive carpet. They move from the
study into the hallway, all the way to the living room. Their
bodies so close it's almost intimate.

                              ROMY
                    Stop! Jesus Christ.

Romy manages to separate them. Both exhausted, the two men
catch their breath. Romy stands in between them.

                              JACOB
                    (under his breath)
                    You sat at my fucking table. You
                    talked to my girls.

Samuel looks at him.

                              JACOB (CONT'D)
                    How long? How fucking long?
                         (to Romy)
                    You lied to me- you fucking lied to
                    me!

Romy tries to keep Samuel calm, who's eyes are dark with
aggression.

                              JACOB (CONT'D)
                    I felt sorry for you!

Jacob pushes Romy away. Samuel can't help but be provoked to
engage again. He pushes Jacob onto the sofa. Jacob tries to
fight back. Samuel attacks him. He throws a punch.

                                                   CUT TO:

Time lapse- they are exhausted. The spotless living room is
now a war-zone. Panting, like tired animals, Samuel and
Jacobd sit in two different corners of the room. Quietly,
Romy comes in and hands each of them a bag of frozen peas.
Samuel holds it against his cheek. He starts to get up.

                              JACOB (CONT'D)
                    Sit down.

He does. They ice their bruises. Jacob studies Samuel's face.

                              JACOB (CONT'D)
                    (strangely calm)
                    She used you. You know that right?
                    She abused you-

Samuel looks at him without blinking. A beat.

                              JACOB (CONT'D)
                    (quietly)
                    You think that's intimacy?

                    SAMUEL
          What?

                    JACOB
          Humiliation- domination,
          submission...whatever they call it-
          It's neurotic-

                    SAMUEL
               (calm)
          You're wrong. You don't understand.

                    JACOB
          Female masochism is a male fantasy,
          a male construct, don't you fucking
          get that?

                    SAMUEL
          That's a dated idea of sexuality.

He falls silent when he sees the desperation in Jacob's eyes.

                    JACOB
          A dated idea?

Samuel just looks at Jacob. He sees pain and panic. Jacob can't help himself. His body starts trembling until it violently shakes. Jacob has a full on panic attack. He grabs his chest, gasps for air. Worried, Romy tries to come closer, grabs his arm.

                    JACOB (CONT'D)
               (to Romy)
          No, not you.

Quickly, Samuel takes a glass of water. He cautiously goes to sit next to him and lets Jacob drink. Slowly Samuel lays his hand on Jacob's back, which seems to calm him down. Then Jacob starts bringing his forehead to Samuel's forehead. Samuel isn't sure if Jacob is going to head-butt him or wants to be comforted by him. Head to head they breathe together. They lock eyes. He sees how Jacob's eyes s fill up with tears. Jacob starts to cry. Samuel looks at him for a long beat and whispers:

                    SAMUEL
          I'm sorry. I'm so sorry.

Careful, Samuel gets up. He stands tall and looks at Romy and Jacob, both sitting on the floor like two children. Calm, he walks to the front door, opens it. Romy and Jacob stare at the door as he walks away, leaving the door open behind him. Light from the morning sun shines through.

PRE-LAB:

> ESME
> It is such a huge honor to have been guided by a woman named Romy Mathis.

INT. OFFICE BUILDING PRESS ROOM DAY

Close on Esme's face in front of a green screen with the Tensile logo behind her. She looks straight at us as she is giving a speech for the company. At the bottom of the screen we read: *Esme Smith, Junior leadership coordinator.*

> ESME
> ...she understands the importance of being a voice for your peers, and an advocate for women around the world who might not have the opportunities that us, sitting here, have.

CUT TO:

EXT. UPSTATE HOUSE- DAY

Romy stands behind the window, trapped and lonely in her doll's house. We hear Esme's speech continue over the images of Romy alone in the house. Time goes by.

> ESME O.S.
> So to be lifted up by a hero like her makes this experience so much more exceptional.

INT. OFFICE BUILDING PRESS ROOM-DAY

Esme looks into the camera and seems to address us directly.

> ESME
> Who are we, as women?

CUT TO:

INT. UPSTATE HOUSE BEDROOM- DAY

With her clothes on, Romy lays awake on the big bed. She holds Nora's teddy bear. Dirty dishes scattered around her. A burning cigarette in her hand. Romy's laptop next to her.

>   ESME O.S.
>   Modern leaders aren't afraid to
>   take chances, embrace change and
>   usher a team into the unknown.

>   CUT TO:

INT. UPSTATE HOUSE HALLWAY- NIGHT

Romy sits on the staircase, her hair a mess, with her phone in her hand, waiting for Jacob to text her.

>   ESME O.S.
>   Sincerity, vulnerability and
>   radical self honesty create a work
>   environment of shared learning,
>   compassion and true connection.

INT OFFICE BUILDING PRESS ROOM DAY

Esme looks into the camera.

>   ESME
>   Now how do we do that? By making
>   changes from top to bottom to
>   support women at every level across
>   the company.

>   CUT TO:

EXT. UPSTATE HOUSE SWIMMING POOL DAY

Wrapped in a blanket, Romy stands at the edge of the pool. She stares into the water. She smokes.

>   ESME O.S.
>   If we dare to let go of expectation
>   and move towards what scares us, we
>   can often find unexpected strength.

Romy throws the cigarette into the pool.

>   ESME O.S. (CONT'D)
>   Today we celebrate genuine
>   authenticity, and true uniqueness
>   in very individual that works at
>   Tensile.

>   CUT TO:

INT. UPSTATE HOUSE- LIVING ROOM- EARLY MORNING

Time has passed. The house is a total mess. Romy is sleeping on the sofa. Dirty plates with cigarette butts and half empty glasses everywhere. The door opens.

              ESME O.S.
We invite each other to show the world who we really are, regardless of peoples assumptions and without fear.

Slowly, Isabel walks in. She looks around. Quickly, she covers her nose with her hand. She kneels down next to her mother and gently touches her face. When Romy opens her eyes, she is surprised to see her daughter.

              ISABEL
        (soft, worried)
Hey- Are you ok? You look like grandma.

              ROMY
How did you get here?

              ISABEL
I took a car.

              ROMY
That's expensive.

Romy smiles.

              ISABEL
Mom, you need to come home. Dad needs you. He refuses to leave the theatre, he doesn't eat, he is reading the bible.

Puzzled, Romy looks at her.

              ISABEL (CONT'D)
He'll forgive you.

Concerned, Romy looks up.

              ROMY
What did he tell you?

              ISABEL
Nothing.

She takes her mother's hand. Ashamed, Romy tries to hide her face.

      ISABEL (CONT'D)
  Mary forgave me.

The sweet comparison touches Romy's heart deeply.

      ISABEL (CONT'D)
   (tears in her eyes)
  It's ok, mom. He'll forgive you.

She hugs her mother.

      ISABEL (CONT'D)
  Come on, lets go home.

INT. THEATER-DAY

Jacob sits alone in the dark and watches the empty stage. The video wall is lowered half way, revealing the back walls of the theatre. Romy enters quietly. She cautiously sits down next to him. He looks frail. He doesn't look at her.

      ROMY
  It's my fault. I told you I was
  someone else, and then I started to
  get angry that you didn't
  understand who I really was. That's
  my- problem, not yours. I'm sorry.
  I'm so sorry.

He looks at her.

EXT. NEW YORK CITY STREETS- DAY

Weeks later. A worker takes down some Christmas decorations.

INT. OFFICE BUILDING ROMY'S OFFICE-DAY

Romy is working on her laptop. Without knocking, Mr. Missel walks into Romy's office.

      MR. MISSEL
  This is a wonderful way to start
  the new year! Huh? How are you
  doing?

She smiles. He sits down. A long beat.

                    MR. MISSEL (CONT'D)
          Mmm—
                (matter of factly)
          Whatever happened to that intern?
          The one that bought me the coffee?

Romy looks up.

                    MR. MISSEL (CONT'D)
          I heard he was recruited by
          Kawasaki, In Tokyo.

                    ROMY
          Wow. Good for him.

                    MR. MISSEL
          Good for you too.

He studies her face.

                    MR. MISSEL (CONT'D)
          You didn't have anything to do with
          that, did you?

She ignores his question.

                    MR. MISSEL (CONT'D)
          Why don't you come over next week
          for drinks and we can talk about it—

She looks at his mouth, his skin. Her tone shifts.

                    ROMY
                (calm)
          Why don't you fuck off, Sebastian?

                    MR. MISSEL
          Careful Romy.

                    ROMY
          I am not afraid of you, of whatever
          the fuck you are capable of, of
          what you know, of what you don't
          know, I don't give a shit. Just
          don't ever talk to me like that
          again. If I want to be humiliated,
          I will pay someone to do it. Now
          get the fuck out of my office.

Romy takes a sip of coffee.

EXT. NEW YORK CITY MORNING

A series of images: Buildings in the mist. Slowly the skies clear. An overhead shot of trees in Central Park. It's Spring. An insect crawling out of the dirt. Birds. Rats. Squirrels.

INT. ROMY AND JACOB'S APARTMENT BEDROOM/ CHEAP HOTEL ROOM DAY

Close on Jacob's face. He looks at Romy full of love. Romy sits opposite him on the bed. She doesn't look away. They stay focused on each other. Both of them are completely vulnerable in this moment. Gently, Romy lays her hand on his heart. A long beat as they keep looking into each others eyes. Jacob smiles, Romy closes her eyes. Slowly, Jacob guides her to lie down on her belly. In his own authentic way, he dominates her. When he lovingly covers her eyes with his hand, allowing her to surrender to herself, we cut to:

<u>In the Cheap Hotel Room with the red walls, Samuel sits on the bed. The dog we saw at the beginning of the film, is in between his legs. Gently, he strokes her head.</u>

Tenderly, Jacob's hands move over Romy's body.

<u>Samuel stands in the middle of the room. The dog circles around Samuel. Elegantly, he lifts his hand as a sign that the dog should sit down. She obeys immediately. She follows Samuel's every move. In his hand he holds a cookie. The dog takes it with her mouth</u>

Jacob uses his fingers to pleasure her. Romy feels safe and seen and is no longer ashamed of the thoughts and images in her head.

<u>Samuel sits on the bed and lovingly holds the dog in his arms. When he slowly gets up, the dog jumps of the bed, following him wherever he goes.</u>

Back to the close up of Romy's face. She starts to orgasm. For real. It's intense and raw. Even though she needed to create a red room in her head, she is closer to Jacob than ever before.

<u>The dog stands next to Samuel. Together, they walk out of the room.</u>

Romy breathes out. She looks into the camera. Liberated.

Printed in Great Britain
by Amazon